NUTSHELLS

INTELLECTUAL PROPERTY LAW IN A NUTSHELL

AUSTRALIA
Law Book Co.
Sydney

CANADA and USA
Carswell
Toronto

HONG KONG
Sweet & Maxwell Asia

NEW ZEALAND
Brookers
Wellington

SINGAPORE and MALAYSIA
Sweet & Maxwell Asia
Singapore and Kuala Lumpur

NUTSHELLS

INTELLECTUAL PROPERTY LAW IN A NUTSHELL

FIRST EDITION

by

CAROLINE WILSON, LL.B., (Hons) (London),
LL.M. (London).
Baker & McKenzie, Lecturer in Intellectual Property
Law,
University of Southampton

London ● Sweet & Maxwell ● 2002

Published in 2002 by
Sweet & Maxwell Limited of
100 Avenue Road, London, NW3 3PF
(http://www.sweetandmaxwell.co.uk)
Typeset by LBJ Typesetting Ltd of Kingsclere
Printed in Great Britain by TJ International Ltd
Padstow, Cornwall

No natural forests were destroyed to make
this product; only farmed timber
was used and replanted

A CIP Catalogue record for this book
is available from the British Library

ISBN 0–421–780002

©
Sweet & Maxwell
2002

CONTENTS

1. INTRODUCTION

WHAT IS INTELLECTUAL PROPERTY?

Intellectual property (IP) is a fast-moving and sometimes complex area of law. Intellectual property rights (IPRs) is the term used to describe the various rights that afford protection to innovative and creative endeavor. The main rights that fall within intellectual property include:

(a) Patents. A patent is a statutory property right that gives the patent owner the exclusive right to use certain inventions.

(b) Breach of confidence. The action for breach of confidence can be used to protect certain categories of confidential information (*e.g.* personal or commercial information) against unauthorised disclosure or use.

(c) Trade marks. Registered trade marks are statutory rights, and give the exclusive right to use a distinctive sign (*e.g.* a name, symbol, scent, jingle, etc.) in relation to a product or service.

(d) Passing off. Goodwill is a form of property constituting the market's perception of the value and quality of a business and its products; this can be protected against interference or damage by passing off. Passing off is a tort that may be used in preventing a trader from making misrepresentations which damages the goodwill of another trader.

(e) Copyright and Moral Rights. Copyright is a statutory right subsisting in original literary, dramatic, musical and artistic works (often known as LDMA works), and, in sound recordings, films, broadcasts, cable programs and the typography of published editions. Owners of copyright have a number of economic rights in their works, including the right to prevent unauthorised copying and adaptation. Moral rights are rights that authors retain in their works, irrespective of who owns the economic rights.

(f) Design law. Certain non-aesthetic and aesthetic aspects of the appearance of articles are protected via a combination of the registered design system, the design right (an unregistered design system) and aspects of copyright law. A registered design is the exclusive right to use certain features of the appearance of a range of products. A design right is the right to prevent the copying of aspects of the shape or configuration of an article such as a manufactured tool. Copyright has a residual role in the field of design law.

Further details and some of the substantive requirements of these IPRs are summarised in the table below:

Outline of Intellectual Property Rights (IPRs)

IPR	Subject Matter of the IPR	Procedure for obtaining the IPR	Duration of IPR
Patent	Novel, industrially applicable inventions capable of an inventive step	A statutory IPR obtained via application to the Patent Office	Up to twenty years
Confidential Information	Government, personal, industrial or trade secrets possessing the necessary quality of confidence	Origins of the action are equitable or contractual	Indefinite, but lasting until the information is released into the public domain
Trade Marks	Distinctive signs capable of being represented graphically	A statutory IPR obtained via application to the Trade Marks Division of the Patent Office	May be renewed indefinitely

IPR	Subject Matter of the IPR	Procedure for obtaining the IPR	Duration of IPR
Passing Off	Protects against misrepresentations damaging the goodwill of an enterprise	A tort	Indefinite, but lasting until the enterprise's goodwill ceases
Copyright	Literary, musical and artistic works, sound recordings, films and broadcasts, etc.	A statutory IPR which arises automatically	Varies. Maximum of the life of the author plus seventy years
Moral rights	The rights to paternity and integrity, the right to object to false attribution in relation to certain copyright works. Also, the right to privacy for photographs and films	Established by statute, moral rights are personal to the author and arise automatically	The rights to paternity, integrity and privacy last for the same period as the relevant copyright. The right to object to false attribution is in place for twenty years from the death of the person subject to the false attribution.
Unregistered Design Right	Aspects of the shape or configuration of articles	A statutory IPR which arises from the recording of the design	Up to fifteen years

IPR	Subject Matter of the IPR	Procedure for obtaining the IPR	Duration of IPR
Registered Design	Aesthetic or functional aspects of the appearance of the whole or part of a product	Application to the Designs Registry of the Patent Office are required for this statutory IPR	Up to twenty-five years

2. REMEDIES FOR IP INFRINGEMENT

INTRODUCTION

In order to be useful, IPRs must be enforced by the right-holder, so it is important to be aware of the range of sanctions and remedies provided for infringement of IPRs.

Generally, IP infringement involves civil remedies, but some criminal sanctions are also available. Final remedies (remedies available after trial) in practice may be less important than interim remedies (remedies awarded at the interim stage, formerly known as the interlocutory stage).

FINAL REMEDIES: PECUNIARY REMEDIES

Financial compensation for losses caused by infringement may take the form of damages or an account of profits.

Account of profits

This is an equitable remedy involving the award to the rightholder of the profits that the defendant has made from the infringement. Account of profits is a discretionary remedy and a rightholder cannot enjoy both damages and account of profits (*Potton v. Yorkclose* (1990)). Where a rightholder has the choice of electing for account of profits, that choice should be an informed one (*Island Records Ltd v. Tring International plc* (1995)).

In *Celanese International Corporation v. BP Chemicals* (1999), guidance as how to calculate an award under account of profits was given:

(i) The first step is to ascertain the total profits possible from the activities of the infringer.
(ii) Then, if appropriate, the total profits should be apportioned to establish the ball point profit (*i.e.* the profit which is attributable to the infringement);
(iii) The resultant figure should then be adjusted to reflect the nature of the parties' cases; and
(iv) Any tax paid should then be deducted.

Damages

An award of damages is the most common pecuniary remedy for IP infringement. Usually damages are calculated on the basis of lost profits or on a royalty basis. Irrespective of the method used, the general rule for is that they should be compensatory; they should put the party back in the position they would have been had the infringement not occurred (*General Tire v. Firestone Tyre* (1975)).

Aggravated damages may also be available. An illustration is the statutory provision for aggravated damages in copyright (CDPA 1988, s.97(2)) and it is clear that such damages may be awarded on a wider basis than at common law, for example aggravated damages may include a restitutionary element (*Nottinghamshire Healthcare NHS Trust v. News Group Newspapers Ltd* (2002)).

FINAL REMEDIES: NON-PECUNIARY REMEDIES

(a) Declaration. Declaratory relief (a declaration of infringement or of non-infringement) is discretionary.
(b) Delivery-up and destruction. In order to ensure that injunctions are properly effective, the court has the equitable power to order the delivery up of infringing articles or documents for destruction, or else to require their destruction under oath by the defendant.
(c) Discovery of names. This is a discretionary disclosure order, known as a Norwich Pharmacal order (after *Norwich Pharmacal* (1974)), which is made to an innocent third party

requiring them to reveal the names of the those that are ultimately responsible for the infringement. Orders for discovery will be made where this is the only way whereby the claimant can identify whom to act against. An order for discovery has been granted against an ISP to disclose the name and address of an individual who had anonymously posted defamatory information on an internet bulletin board (*Totalise Plc v. The Motely Fool Ltd and another* (2002)); the judge noted that the order was necessary in the interests of justice, as otherwise individuals could utilise the internet to defame with impunity.

(d) Injunction. An injunction is a Court Order. They are equitable remedies given at the Court's discretion. There has been some dispute as to the appropriate breadth of final injunctions; the normal final injunction (*i.e.* not to infringe the IPR at issue) had been felt to be too broad and more specific injunctions have been favoured (*Microsoft v. Plato* (1999)). More recently, the Court of Appeal has cast doubt on the appropriateness of so called narrow final injunctions (*Coflexip v. Stolt* (2001)). Injunctions are also available at the interim stage (see below).

INTERIM REMEDIES

Interim injunctions

An interim injunction can often provide the only effective remedy to an IP rightholder. This, and the fact that most IP infringement disputes do not progress beyond the interim stage, ensures that interim injunctions are particularly important in IP law.

The standard guidance as to when an interim injunction should be granted was set out in *American Cyanamid v. Ethicon* (1975):

(a) The claimant should have an arguable case;
(b) Damages would not provide an adequate remedy; and
(c) The courts should consider the balance of commercial convenience. If this is equal, the courts should act to preserve the *status quo*.

The *American Cyanamid* formula was criticised in *Series 5 Software v. Clarke* (1996) where the discretionary nature of interim relief and the importance of examining the merits of the case where emphasised. The availability of interim injunctions has also been affected by the increasing impact of human rights considerations (most recently in *A v. B and Another* (2002)) and so the current position is somewhat more restrictive than the *American Cyanamid* formula suggests, and might be re-stated as follows:

(a) The claimant should have an arguable case except, as *per A v. B and C plc* (2002), in breach of confidence cases where issues of freedom of expression are at stake, in which case the slightly higher standard of the claimant being likely to succeed at trial should apply.

(b) The courts should consider the extent to which damages are likely to be an adequate remedy, and also consider the ability of the parties to pay (*Series 5 Software v. Clarke* (1996)).

(c) The courts should consider the balance of commercial convenience. If this is equal, the courts should act to preserve the *status quo*. In breach of confidence cases where an issue of freedom of expression is at stake, as *per A v. B and C plc* (2002), the court should weigh up the claim based on freedom of expression as against the claimant's position. If, as in *A v. B and C plc* (2002), the claimant invokes a claim of privacy, the court should weigh the claim to privacy as against that of the claim to freedom of expression and an injunction should only be granted here where it is justified.

Ex parte orders

Inter partes proceedings (now known as proceedings on notice) are proceedings where the defendant has been served and has had sufficient time to prepare his defence. In contrast, *ex parte* hearings (know known as proceedings without notice) is a hearing where only one side is represented (as *per Intergraph v. Solid Systems* (1993), this party is under a duty of full and frank disclosure). *Ex parte* orders preserve the *status quo* pending a full hearing. There are two such orders which are of relevance:

(a) Search orders. These were formerly known as Anton Piller Orders after *Anton Piller* (1976), the case where the first such order was granted. The grant of a search order allows the premises of an alleged infringer to be searched and evidence of infringement to be seized. The courts have developed safeguards against the abuse of search orders (*Universal Thermosensors v. Hibben* (1992)), for example, the applicant must be able to demonstrate a strong *prima facie* case of infringement. There must also be a likelihood of real and serious damage, clear evidence that there are documents or property at the alleged infringer's site and a serious possibility that they will be destroyed if the alleged infringer is put on notice. Other safeguards include that the order must be carried out by an experienced independent solicitor, documents cannot be removed and where possible, the order must be carried out on business premises during business hours.

(b) Freezing injunction. These were formerly known as Mareva injunctions. These injunctions freeze the assets of an alleged infringer pending a full trial (*Mareva* (1975)), thus preventing the alleged infringer from transferring assets out of the jurisdiction.

CRIMINAL SANCTIONS

Generally, IP infringement involves civil remedies, but some criminal sanctions are available. For the statutory IPRs, the individual statutes provide for criminal sanctions, *e.g.* Copyright, Designs and Patents Act 1988, s.107 provides for imprisonment and fines for secondary infringement. Also there is the general common law crime of conspiracy to defraud may be used in order to protect IPRs.

THREATS

Groundless threats to sue for IP infringement may in themselves be actionable (see, *e.g.* s.70, Patent Act 1977, s.70, Registered Designs Act 1949, s.26 and Trade Mark Act 1994, s.21).

3.　PATENT LAW

INTRODUCTION

What is a patent?

Patents are monopoly rights. Products or processes may be patented but irrespective of the form of the patent, the product or process must satisfy the substantive criteria of the Patents Act 1977 (PA 1977). These are:

(i) There must be an *invention*, but *not an "as such" invention or a non-patentable invention* (PA 1977, s.1(2) and (3));
(ii) *Novelty* must be present (PA 1977, s.2);
(iii) An *inventive step* must be present (PA 1977, s.3); and
(iv) The invention must be capable of *industrial application* (PA 1977, s.4).

OBTAINING A PATENT

A patent is a territorial right, so it is necessary to apply for a patent in each jurisdiction for which protection is desired, *e.g.* a UK patent may be obtained from the UK Patent Office. There is currently no "European patent" (a single patent valid in all EU member states), but a "bundle" of national patents from states that are party to the European Patent Convention 1973 (EPC) may be obtained from a single patent application to the European Patent Office (EPO). Because of this and the fact that the PA 1977 is based on the EPC 1973, EPO decisions are of interest to UK patent lawyers.

NOT INVENTIONS "AS SUCH"

The statute does not provide a definition of "invention', but PA 1977, s.1(2) sets out a list of things that are considered not to be inventions "as such". Generally, abstract, aesthetic and non-technical things are considered to be excluded thing "as such".

Discoveries, scientific theories and mathematical methods

Discoveries, scientific theories and mathematical methods are not inventions "as such" (PA 1977, s.1(2)(a)). It has been suggested that a discovery is a disclosure that adds to the amount of human knowledge, whereas an invention necessarily also suggests an act to be done (*Reynolds v. Smith* (1913)). The line between discovery and invention can be difficult to draw, but it is clear that a "mere" discovery must be developed and applied in some way before it constitutes an invention. The same principle holds true for scientific theories and mathematical methods; on their own they are unpatentable, but where they have a technical effect or make a technical contribution (*Fujitsu* (1997)), they will be patentable.

Aesthetic creations

Literary, dramatic, musical and artistic works or any other aesthetic creation are not inventions "as such" (PA 1977, s.1(2)(b)), as they are protected by copyright.

Computer programs

PA 1977, s.1(2)(c) lists a number of things that are not regarded as being inventions "as such", and one of the most problematic things included in this list is computer programs. Despite s.1(2)(c), patents for software-related inventions are in fact granted. Software patents are granted where a *substantive technical contribution* is made (this concept derives from a line of EPO decisions from *Vicom's Application* (1987), onwards) as this is not considered to be a computer programs "as such". In deciding whether there is a technical contribution, one of two approaches may be taken:

(a) One should ask whether technical means are used to produce a result or solve a problem; or
(b) One should ask whether the invention produces a technical result.

Although there has been some criticism of the substantive technical contribution approach (*e.g.* see *Fujitsu Ltd's Application* (1977)), the UK courts have followed the EPO. Recent changes to UK Patent Office practice (following changes made by the EPO after *IBM's Application* (1999)) mean that claims to computer programs, either themselves or on a carrier (*e.g.* on a floppy disc or CD-ROM), are accepted provided that the program is such that when run on a computer, it produces a technical effect. At the time of writing a draft directive relating to the patentability of computer programs was under consideration and this development should result in further harmonisation with the EPO approach.

A scheme, rule or method for performing a mental act, playing a game or business methods

The following are not patentable "as such" (PA 1977, s.1(2)(c)):

(i) Mental acts. In *Raytheon* (1993) an apparatus and process was claimed for the identification of ships; this involved the digital comparison of the silhouette of the unknown ship with silhouettes of known ships held in a computer memory. The claim was held to be excluded as it was merely an automation of a method normally carried out by individuals, *i.e.* a mental act as such. Carrying out this method with a computer did not create a technical effect.
(ii) Schemes, rules or methods for playing a game. It is difficult to see how innovations in this area could be said to be making a technical contribution. For example, a blue

coloured squash ball might add desirable characteristics to play such as enhanced visual impact and thus a competitive advantage (*ITS Rubber* (1979)), but such advantages do not amount to a technical contribution.

(iii) Business methods. The UK courts have traditionally taken a strict approach to the patentability of business methods—inventions must make a technical contribution but that contribution must not be in an excluded thing (such as a business method), and, in any case advances in the field of business are not technical (*Merill Lynch's Application* (1989)). More recently, EPO developments indicate that a more relaxed approach may be adopted. Whilst *process* claims to business methods are not inventions "as such", *product claims* may be patentable—"a computer suitably programmed for use in a particular field, even business is a concrete apparatus as in a physical entity, man-made for a utilitarian purpose and is therefore an invention" (*PBS PARTNERSHIP/Pension Benefits System* (2000)). It should be noted that as in *Pension Benefits System*, in practice many modern business methods involve use of computer programs.

The presentation of information

PA 1977, s.1(2)(d) provides that means of presenting information are not inventions "as such". Under old patent legislation, navigation apparatus and use of navigational aids have been found to fall foul of the equivalent of s.1(2)(d) (*Loth* (1924) and *W's Application* (1914)).

NON-PATENTABLE INVENTIONS

In the rare circumstances where the commercial exploitation of an invention would be contrary to public policy or morality, that invention would be unpatentable (PA 1977, s.1(3)). The EPO in *HARVARD/Onco-Mouse* (1991), when considering the patentability of a mouse or other non-human mammal genetically engineered so as to be pre-disposed to develop cancer, suggested that this should be addressed via a balancing exercise. Here, the suffering of the Onco-mouse and the possible environmental risks were felt to be outweighed by the utility of the invention to humans, hence the Onco-Mouse was not immoral.

As public policy and morality objections proved particularly problematic in the field of biotechnology, Directive 98/44/EC on the Legal Protection of Biotechnological Invention (see Schedule A2 Biotechnological Inventions, Patents Act 1977) provides further guidance as to what is not patentable:

(i) The formation and development of the human body and mere discoveries of elements of the human body (this includes gene sequences) are not patentable. However, where a *technical process* is used to isolate or produce elements (including genes) from the human body, this may be patentable.

(ii) Processes for modifying human germ line genetic identity (*i.e.* genetic changes that can be passed to the next generation).

(iii) Human cloning processes.

(iv) Genetic engineering of animals which is likely to cause the animal to suffer without a substantial medical benefit, either to man or animals (this "weighing up" approach is the same as that used in the *Onco-Mouse* decision).

(v) Plant or animal varieties or biological processes for the production of such varieties are not patentable, but inventions concerning plants or animals may be patented where the invention is *not confined to a particular variety*. This is a very narrow view of the concept of "variety" but it is consistent with EPO decisions in cases such as *NOVARTIS/ Transgenic Plant* (1999) and *HARVARD/Onco-Mouse* (1991)).

NOVELTY

An invention must be novel (PA 1977, s.1(1)(a)). In UK patent law, the terms *novelty* and *anticipation* are used interchangeably.

The novelty test

The invention must be new in the sense that it must not previously have been made available to the public. PA 1977, s.2(1) provides that an invention is novel where it does not form part of the state of the art.

Anticipation is judged by asking *is the invention part of the state of the art?* Novelty is assessed objectively.

In order for an invention to be anticipated, the prior art must either contain an *enabling disclosure* (in the case of a product patent), or, for process patents it must give *clear and unmistakable directions to do what the applicant has invented* (*General Tire* (1972)).

The state of the art

PA 1977, s.2(2) defines the state of the art as comprising all matter made available to the public before the priority date of the invention (the priority date is the date of the first patent application). It therefore comprises all knowledge (worldwide) on the subject matter of the invention; this knowledge can be made available in any way—whether by written means (publication) oral transmission, use (*e.g. Windsurfing v. Tabor Marine* (1985)) or by any other means before the priority date.

The state of the art includes matter included in earlier patent applications, including those patent applications that are not yet published (PA 1977, s.2(3)). Everything in the state of the art is known as *prior art*. Novelty-destroying prior art could include information that is part of common general knowledge (*Buhler v. Satake* (1997)) as well as specific pieces of prior art.

Novel new uses

In some circumstances, a known invention may still be patented where a new use for that invention is found:

(a) First medical use. The PA 1977 provides that the first medical use of a known compound is novel, provided that the medical application of the compound does not itself form part of the state of the art (PA 1977, s.2(6)).

(b) Second medical use. In Europe, a practice has developed of allowing second and subsequent medical uses of known compounds (*EISAI/Second Medical Indication* (1985)). Such claims are novel where the second or subsequent medical use does not form part of the state of the art, and, provided the patent application itself takes a very narrow form known as a Swiss Form claim, *i.e.* the "use of Medicament X for the treatment of Disease Y". The UK courts have sanctioned the use of Swiss Form claims, but second and subsequent medical uses will only be novel in the UK where there is a new therapeutic application; discovering further information about a known medical use is insufficient (*Bristol-Myers Squibb v. Baker Norton Pharmaceuticals* (2001)).

(c) Second (non-medical) use. It is also possible for new uses of known things to be novel in the non-medical field where they are directed towards a new use that is sufficiently different so as not to be regarded as being part of the state of the art. This is assessed by asking: *has the claimed functional technical feature been previously been made available to the public?* (*MOBIL/Friction Reducing Additive* (1990)). In *MOBIL*, a compound previously used as a rust-preventing additive was successfully patented for use for the purpose of reducing friction. The friction-reducing qualities of the compound were the functional technical feature and as the compound has only previously been known and used for rust-prevention, this use was novel. *MOBIL*-type reasoning is recognised in the UK but has, nevertheless, been subject to some criticism (*e.g.* in *Merrill Dow v. Norton* (1996)).

INVENTIVE STEP

A patentable invention must involve an inventive step; an inventive step is present where the invention would not be obvious to a person skilled in the art (PA 1977, s.3). In patent law, the terms *inventive step* and *non-obviousness* are used interchangeably.

Inventive step is a very different question from that of novelty. For the purposes of inventive step, the relevant prior art (*i.e.* the state of the art) is slightly different from as that for novelty (see above); unpublished patent applications do not form part of the state of the art for the purposes of inventive step (PA 1977, s.3). More fundamentally, inventive step is a *qualitative* question as opposed to the *quantitative* nature of novelty.

The skilled man

Inventive step are assessed from the perspective of the person skilled in the art (PA 1977, s.3); the skilled man. This notional figure has certain attributes; he is the average person in the relevant art, possessing the relevant skills, knowledge and qualifications (*Technograph Printed Circuits v. Mills* (1972)). Where research in the relevant art would be carried out by a research team, the viewpoint of the notional research team will instead by adopted (*Genetech* (1989)). There is some questioning as to whether the skilled man is entirely uninventive (*e.g.* Mustill L.J. and Purchas L.J. in *Genetech* (1989)), but it would seem that that is indeed the case (*PLG Research v. Ardon International* (1995)).

The *Windsurfer* test

The statutory test for inventive step has been structured into what is known as the *Windsurfer* test; this test follows the approach set out in *Windsurfing v. Tabur Marine* (1985), as modified by *PLG Research Ltd v. Ardon International Ltd* (1995). According to the *Windsurfer* test, in order to assess obviousness one should ask:

(i) What is the inventive step involved in the patent?
(ii) At the priority date, what was the state of the art relevant to that step?
(iii) How does the step differ from the state of the art?
(iv) Without hindsight, would the taking of that step be obvious to the person skilled in the art?

The structured approach of the *Windsurfer* test was considered by the Court of Appeal in a recent case to be useful, but not essential (*David John Instance v. Denny Bros. Printing Ltd.* 2001)). Despite this, and the fact that the EPO use a very different approach to inventive step (the "problem and solution" approach), *Windsurfer* continues to be primary test for inventive step in the UK.

Secondary considerations

Some things are clearly obvious, *e.g.* a combination of two known machines with no resultant improvement in function will be obvious (*Williams v. Nye* (1890)). Assessment of obviousness is often more difficult, however, and other tests may be useful. Where other obviousness tests are used with *Windsurfer*, they are known as secondary considerations. Secondary considerations are used in a supplementary role to inform the fourth element of the *Windsurfer* test (*Mölnlycke AB v. Procter & Gamble Ltd (No. 1)* (1990)).

A number of obviousness tests have been used over the years but the following are particularly interesting as secondary considerations:

(i) Commercial success. The relevance of commercial success to obviousness was traditionally doubted, as commercial success can flow from factors other than inventiveness (*e.g.* advertising). However, the commercial success of the invention may now be a material factor in determining whether the new result was obvious or not (*Haberman v. Jackal International* (1999)), particularly where that invention meets a long-felt want.

(ii) The "worthwhile to try" test. This test was strictly applied in *Genetech* (1989). In *Biogen v. Medeva* (1997) a less stringent approach was advocated.

INDUSTRIAL APPLICATION

The invention must be capable of being applied in industry (PA 1977, s.4). Virtually all inventions bar those that are theoretically impossible (*e.g.* perpetual motion machines) can be said to meet this requirement; it is the exclusions to industrial applicability that can cause difficulties.

Methods of treatment of the human or animal body including surgery, therapy or diagnosis are deemed not to be capable of industrial application (PA 1977, s.4(2)). As substances or equipment used in medical treatment are capable of industrial application (PA 1977, s.4(3)), this leads to the distinction between methods of treatment and products used in treatment. So, an anaesthetic drug and anaesthetic equipment might be patentable but the dosage regime employed in using the anaesthetic drug and surgical techniques would not be patentable.

OWNERSHIP OF PATENTS AND THE EMPLOYEE INVENTOR

The basic rules are that a patent may be granted to the following:

   (i) The inventor or joint inventors, *i.e.* the actual deviser(s) of the invention (PA 1977, s.7(2)(a));
  (ii) The inventor(s)' successors in title; or
 (iii) The employer of an employee inventor (see below).

Ownership of employee inventions

Inventors have the right to be mentioned as such (PA 1977, s.13), but PA 1977, s.39(1) provides that where inventors are employees (see PA 1977, s.130), their employer will own the invention if:

  (a) The invention was made in the course of the employee's normal duties (*e.g. Harris' Patent* (1985)) or in the course of specially assigned duties, provided he/she might reasonably be expected to carry those duties out (*e.g. Electrolux v. Hudson* (1977)), or
  (b) Where the employee has a special obligation to further the interests of his employer's undertaking. This is related to the duty of fidelity that employees owe their employers; typically, the more senior the employee, the greater the scope of this obligation and the more likely that the employer will own the invention.

Compensation for employee inventors

Where the invention belongs to the employer (PA 1977, s.39(1)), statutory compensation of the employee inventor may be available (PA 1977, s.40), provided that:

(i) The patent is of outstanding benefit to the employer;
(ii) The invention is subject of a patent grant; and
(iii) It is just that compensation be awarded.

The threshold for statutory compensation is very high and there has never been a reported case where statutory compensation under the PA 1977 has been awarded (such disputes tend to be settled out of court).

SUFFICIENCY

Patent applications may fail or granted patents subsequently may be revoked (PA 1977, s.72(1)(c)) on the basis of sufficiency. A patent application has a number of components and the patent specification is a vital part in which the invention is described and defined, it is the source of all the information about the patent that reached the public domain.

The specification must disclose the invention in such a way that the invention could be performed by the person skilled in the art (PA 1977, s.14(3)), i.e. the application must contain an enabling disclosure (*Biogen v. Medeva* (1997)).

Patent claims themselves determine the scope of the monopoly granted to a patent proprietor. Claims must be clear and concise, be supported by the description and relate to a single inventive concept (PA 1977, s.14(5))

INFRINGEMENT

The following activities carried out in the UK without the consent of the patent proprietor, constitute patent infringement:

(a) Primary infringement. This falls into three categories:
(i) PA 1977, s.60(1)(a), where a *product patent* is at issue, making, disposing of, offering to dispose of, using, importing or keeping the patented product (for disposal or otherwise).
(ii) PA 1977, s.60(1)(b), where a *process patent* is at issue, use of the process with actual or constructive knowledge that non-consensual use constitutes infringement.

(iii) PA 1977, s.60(1)(c). The use, offer to dispose of, importation or keeping (for disposal or otherwise) of a product directly obtained from a patented process. However, where intermediate steps are necessary the defendant's product will not infringe the claimant's process patent (*Pioneer Electronics v. Warner Music Manufacturing* (1995)).

(b) Contributory infringement (s.60(2)). The supply or offer to supply any of the means that relate to an essential element of the invention, for putting the invention into effect may constitute infringement. This will only be the case where there is actual or constructive knowledge that these means are suitable (and are intended) for putting the invention into effect in the UK.

Proceedings for patent infringement may be brought by the exclusive licensee as well as by the patent proprietor (PA 1977, s.67(1)).

Exceptions to infringement

There are a number of exceptions to patent infringement set out in PA 1977, s.60(5)(a)–(f). The main exceptions are:

(a) Private and non-commercial use (PA 1977, s.60(5)(a)).
(b) Experimental use (PA 1977, s.60(5)(b)).

The courts have considered whether repairs to patented products constitute patent infringement a number of times. The position (as set out in *British Leyland v. Armstrong* (1986)) is relatively clear; genuine repair of a patented product that has been sold for use with the consent of the proprietor does not constitute infringement, only repair that amounts to reconstruction will infringe. The boundary between making a product (which constitutes infringement) and repairing a product (which falls outside) is to be judged objectively (*United Wire Ltd v. Screen Repair Services (Scotland) Ltd & Another* (2001)).

Finally, there are limited prior user rights. A person who made use of an invention before its priority date may continue to use that invention, subject to certain restrictions (PA 1977, s.64).

Counterclaim for revocation

An opponent can attack a patent by counterclaiming for revocation of the patent. The grounds for revocation are:

(i) Not a patentable invention PA 1977, s.72(1)(a)), *i.e.* the subject matter of the patent is not an invention "as such" or the invention is contrary to public policy or morality, or has been anticipated, is obvious or is not industrially applicable;
(ii) Non-entitlement (PA 1977, s.72(1)(b)). The person granted the patent is not the person entitled to the patent;
(iii) Insufficiency (PA 1977, s.72(1)(c)). The patent specification does not amount to an enabling disclosure; or
(iv) Impermissible amendment (PA 1977, s.72(1)(d) and (e)). The protection afforded by the patent has been extended by an amendment that should not have been allowed.

Claim interpretation

To establish infringement, the allegedly infringing act must fall within the scope of the patent claims. This can be difficult to determine where the allegedly infringing product or process is a variant of the patented product or process. Claim interpretation involves establishing the scope of the monopoly claimed and the required approach is set out in PA 1977, s.125; this requires compliance with the Protocol to the Interpretation of Art 69 EPC. The Protocol requires EPC member states to interpret patent claims not in a strict literal way, nor in such a way that the patent claims are viewed as mere guidelines, but a position should be adopted between these two extremes so as to ensure fairness for the patentee and certainty for third parties.

It is not entirely certain as to whether the UK's approach to claim interpretation, the purposive approach (first stated in *Catnic Components v. Hill Smith* (1982) and reworked in *Improver Corporation v. Consumer Products* (1990)), is consistent with the Protocol (*e.g.* see *PLG Research v. Ardon International Ltd* (1995)). The purposive approach (*Catnic* as restated in *Improver*) is as follows:

(i) Had the variant a material effect on the manner the invention works?
(ii) If not, would this have been obvious?
(iii) If yes, would the reader understand that strict compliance with the wording of the invention was required by the patentee?
(iv) If yes, the variant is outside the claim.

The third element of the test has often been applied in an inconsistent manner (*e.g.* see the varying approaches employed by the judges in *Wheatley v. Drillsafe* (2001).

Remedies

Remedies are discussed in general in Chapter 2. The following remedies are available for patent infringement:

  (i) Injunction (PA 1977, s.61(1)(a)).
 (ii) An order for delivery-up or destruction (PA 1977, s.61(1)(b)).
(iii) Damages *or* account of profits (PA 1977, s.61(1)(c) and (d)), but no damages or account shall be ordered where the infringer had no reasonable grounds for supposing that the patent existed (PA 1977, s.62(1)).
 (iv) Declaration of that the patent is valid and not infringed (PA 1977, s.61(1)(e)).

A declaration, injunction and damages are also available where a groundless threat of patent infringement (PA 1977. s.70)) is made.

CRIMINAL SANCTIONS

Provision for criminal sanctions is made in PA 1977, ss.110-111.

4. BREACH OF CONFIDENCE

INTRODUCTION

The action for breach of confidence has its origins in equity and contract. It can operate as a supplementary action, supporting as an action for patent infringement for example, or it can form an action by itself. The law of confidence protects all qualifying confidences in the private, governmental and commercial arenas, but different policy considerations are likely to affect the scope of protection within each of these three "categories" of confidential information.

Privacy—the impact of the Human Rights Act 1998

Traditionally, there was no right to privacy in the UK (*Kaye v. Robertson* (1991)). With the introduction of the Human Rights

Act 1998, English law now recognises the right to privacy in accordance with Article 8 European Convention on Human Rights (this was first explicitly stated in *Douglas v. Hello!* (2001)). This right must, however, be balanced against Article 10 of the European Convention on Human Rights (ECHR) which guarantees freedom of expression (*Douglas v. Hello!* (2001)).

In *Douglas v. Hello!* (2001), the Court of Appeal in its interim judgement noted that there are differing degrees of privacy, and that in this case a major part of Michael Douglas' and Catherine Zeta-Jones' right to privacy in their wedding had been sold in a commercial transaction.

A v. B and C plc (2002) concerned the freedom of the Sunday People newspaper to publish the identity of the participants in a "kiss and tell" story involving a Premiership footballer (A). It was confirmed that there was *no new tortious cause of action that protected privacy*, the action for breach of confidence must provide a remedy instead. The court helpfully set out the principles that should govern the availability of interim relief in breach of confidence where there are privacy and freedom of expression issues (these principles are summarised in Chapter 2, above). Great emphasis was placed on the freedom of the Press; it is not enough for the claimant merely demonstrate that there is no public interest in publication, he/she must demonstrate that any interference in the freedom of the Press must be justified. The weaker the claim to privacy or the greater the public interest in publication, the more likely it is that an interim injunction to restrain publication will not be granted. In this case, such considerations were not relevant as the case for breach of confidence was not made out; the affairs did not attract the necessary quality of confidence (see below).

In *Naomi Campbell v. Mirror Group Newspapers* (2002), it was again confirmed that *Douglas v. Hello!* (2001) and *A v. B and C plc* were correct; whilst UK law recognises a right to privacy, there is no separate tort of privacy and breach of confidence must be expanded so as to accommodate privacy.

Further discussion of the role of human rights in breach of confidence and the status and scope of privacy are likely in future cases.

Elements of the action for breach of confidence

The key case in breach of confidence is *Coco v. Clarke* (1969), in which Mr Justice Megarry established the essential elements for a successful action in breach of confidence. Here, the claimant had disclosed details as to the design and proposals for manufacture of a moped engine. After some disagreements, the defendants proceeded to manufacture their own engine and the claimant applied for an interim injunction to restrain the defendants using information that he had been disclosed. The claimant failed. To succeed, the relevant information must have the necessary quality of confidence, the information must be communicated in circumstances importing an obligation of confidence, and, there must be unauthorised use of the information (the claimant only satisfied the second element of this test).

ELEMENTS OF THE ACTION OF BREACH OF CONFIDENCE: THE NECESSARY QUALITY OF CONFIDENCE

Introduction

The information may take any form; a verbal disclosure, in writing, via a drawing, *etc.* Etchings were held to have the necessary quality of confidence in *Prince Albert v. Strange* (1849), as was the genetic information contained in nectarine budwood in an Australian case (*Franklin v. Giddins* (1978)).

The mere fact that the information is encrypted seems to be insufficient on its own to succeed in an action for breach of confidence (the other two elements of the action must still be satisfied, *Mars UK Ltd v. Teknowledge Ltd* (2000)).

Types of information

There are no limitations to the type of information that can be protected by the law of confidence. The action can be used for trade secrets, government secrets and to protect personal secrets:

(a) Commercial secrets, *e.g. Seager v. Copydex (No. 1)* (1967) concerned commercial information.
(b) Government secrets. *e.g. A-G v. Guardian Newspapers (No. 2) "Spycatcher"* (1990) concerned government information.
(c) Personal secrets. Whether an individual's Narcotics Anonymous treatment is confidential was considered in *Campbell v. MGN* (2002). Information arising out of marriage and stable other relationships is afforded more protection than is information from transient personal relationships (*A v. B and C plc* (2002)).

There are two exceptions to the general principle that any type of information can be protected by the action of breach of confidence:

(i) The courts will not protect "trivial tittle tattle" (*Coco v. Clarke* (1969)). What constitutes trivial information is unclear, but this must be a very narrow category as the courts have afforded protection to information without any apparent commercial value.

(ii) Immorality. The courts should not act as censors or arbiters of taste (*A v. B and C plc* (2002)).

"The necessary quality of confidence"

For information to have the necessary quality of confidence, it must not be public property or knowledge (*Saltman Engineering v. Campbell Engineering* (1948)). So, once the information is in the public domain, it cannot generally be regarded as being confidential. Yet, information need not be absolutely confidential in order to have the necessary quality of confidence; relative secrecy may suffice, as confidentiality is a matter of degree (*Franchi v. Franchi* (1967)). The information must be clearly identifiable, and be sufficiently well developed so as to be capable of realisation (*De Maudsley v. Palumbo* (1996)).

ELEMENTS OF THE ACTION FOR BREACH OF CONFIDENCE: THE OBLIGATION OF CONFIDENCE

There must be an obligation of confidence arising from the circumstances in which the information was imparted (*Coco v. A.N. Clarke (Engineering) Ltd*) (1969)). The obligation need not be express, as the courts have been prepared to imply an obligation of confidence in certain circumstances (*e.g.* in *Ackroyds v. Islington Plastics* (1962)), the court held that there had been a breach of an implied contractual term and a duty of confidence to use the information (in the shape of a tool) only for the purposes for which it was supplied.)

Circumstances giving rise to an obligation of confidence

Each of the circumstances that could give rise to an obligation of confidence shall be examined in turn:

(a) From contract. Where there is express contractual provisions as to confidentiality, the terms of the contract will
dictate as to whether an obligation is imposed. Where, as
in *Fraser v. Evans* (1969), there is no express reciprocal
duty, none will be implied.
(b) From an existing relationship. An obligation might arise
from:
    (i) Commercial Relationships. In pre-existing commer-
cial relationships, an obligation may be implied.
Traditionally, this has been regarded as an objective
question, *i.e.* on the basis of the understanding of the
reasonable man (*Coco v. A.N. Clarke (Engineering) Ltd*
(1969)). This is probably the preferred approach,
despite Mr Justice Jacob's assertion in *Carflow Products v. Linwood Securities* (1996), that the equitable
nature of the law of confidence suggests a subjective
approach.
    (ii) Employment relationships. Here, duties of confi-
dence are particularly significant and due to the
differing interests of ex-employees and their former
employers, a major distinction is drawn between the
extent of the obligation implied for current as
opposed to former employees.
        The main case in this area is *Faccenda Chickens v.
Fowler* (1987). Here it was said that where there is or
was a contract of employment, the contract deter-
mines the extent of employee's obligations. If there
are no express term, then implied terms including
the duty of good faith or fidelity will be imposed on
the employee. *Hivac Ltd v. Park Royal Scientific Instruments Ltd* (1946) provides that the duty of fidelity
involves not only the protection of commercial
secrets, but also a duty not to compete with the
employer (legitimate preparation to compete is
permitted).
        The ex-employee is less restricted. The implied
term only extends to protecting information so
highly confidential so it to amount to a trade secret
(*Faccenda Chickens v. Fowler* (1987)).
(c) Professional relationships. Professional advisors owe an
obligation to those that they advise.
(d) Statute. Relevant statutory provisions include the Official
Secrets Act 1989 and CDPA 1988, s.85.

Status of the third party recipient of confidential information

As a general rule a third party who is in possession of information which he knows is confidential, is subject to an obligation of confidence (*Prince Albert* (1849)). There is some debate as to what constitutes sufficient knowledge for the conscience of the third party to be bound, but the innocent recipient is clearly not bound by an obligation of confidence (*Valeo Vision v. Flexible Lamps* (1995)).

ELEMENTS OF THE ACTION FOR BREACH OF CONFIDENCE: UNAUTHORISED USE

This is the third element of the *Coco* test. There must be actual or threatened use of the confidential information, in breach of the obligation of confidence.

Intent is irrelevant as to unauthorised use, an objective approach (*Sir Elton John & Ors v. Countess Joulebine* (2001)) is taken and there is no need for the breach to be deliberate or unconscious. In *Seager* (1967), the claimant was in breach of his obligation of confidence, despite acting honestly. So-called subconscious use also constitutes use (as *per Seager* (1967)).

DEFENCES

(i) Lapse of time (as breach of confidence is an equitable action, see *Peter Pan Manufacturing Corp v. Corsets Silhouette Ltd* (1964)).

(ii) Information is in the public domain. Here the information is no longer confidential. An example is *Mustad v. Dosen*, where the claimant disclosed previously secret information by publishing them in a patent application.

(iii) The public interest defence. Traditionally, a very narrow definition of public interest was adopted (*e.g. Initial Services v. Putterill* (1967)), but in *Lion Laboratories v. Evans* (1985), a more general public interest in the preservation of confidences was be outweighed by a countervailing public interest in favour of disclosure. The courts have always recognised that there is a wide difference between what is interesting to the public and what is in the public interest to make known. This distinction appears to have been blurred by Lord Woolf in *A v. B and C plc* (2002), who seemed to depart from the usual public interest test in holding that the test should be what the public *want to know* and what they have a *legitimate interest* to know, rather than what they *need to know*.

REMEDIES

Remedies are discussed in general in Chapter 2. The following remedies are available to an action for breach of confidence:

(i) Injunctions.
(ii) Damages (*e.g. Seager* (1967)).
(iii) Account of profits, *e.g. Peter Pan Manufacturing Corp v. Corsets Silhouette Ltd* (1964).
(iv) Delivery-up, modification or destruction upon oath.

In addition, there is the *springboard doctrine*. If confidential information is put in the public domain, the person who owed the duty may be prevented from using that information for a period of time, he cannot use his breach of confidence as a "springboard" to launch own project, *e.g. Terrapin Ltd v. Builders Supply Co (Hayes) Ltd* (1967).

5. TRADE MARK LAW

INTRODUCTION

Function of trade marks

The function of an ordinary trade mark is to act as an indicator of trade origin, this aids both consumers of branded goods and the trade mark proprietor as follows:

(i) The trade mark acts as an indicator of quality and reliability, protecting consumers from confusion or deception in the marketplace.
(ii) The trade mark can be enforced to protect the mark's proprietor against certain acts of unfair competition.

Collective marks and certification marks

Although rare, such trade marks perform different functions as compared to ordinary trade marks.

Certification marks (TMA 1994, s.50) are intended to indicate that goods or services comply with a certain objective standards as to quality, origin, material, the mode of manufacture of goods or the performance of services or other characteristics. Any third party whose goods or services meet the requisite standards may apply to be an authorised user of a certification mark and the proprietor cannot refuse this request.

Collective marks serve to indicate members of an association. A third party who is not a member of that association does not have the right to use the mark. Collective marks can act as certification marks and *vice versa*.

Trade mark law

In the UK, trade marks are governed by the Trade Marks Act 1994 (TMA 1994), which implements the European Council Directive No 89/104/EEC. An application for a national trade mark may be made to the Trade Mark Registry (part of the UK Patent Office). Community trade marks (CTM), a trade mark that is valid in the entire EU, may be obtained from the CTM Office—the Office for Harmonisation in the Internal Market (Trade Marks and Designs) (OHIM).

Not all marks are capable of being registered as trade marks. Objections to the registration of a mark may be raised, either by the Trade Marks Registry during examination or by third parties during opposition proceedings. The grounds for refusing registration are divided into two categories:

(a) *Absolute grounds* for refusal (TMA 1994, s.3 and 4), which are concerned with objections based on the mark itself.
(b) *Relative grounds* for refusal (TMA 1994, s.5), these are concerned with a conflict with third party rights.

Classification of marks

The Nice Agreement for the International Classification of Goods and Services provides that there are thirty-four classes of goods and eight classes of services. Any application for registration must stipulate which classes, or sub-classes, in which registration is sought. Multi-class applications are possible and it would theoretically be possible to register a mark in respect of all forty-two classes, but this is unlikely as applicants must have a *bona fide* intent to use the mark for the proscribed goods and services (TMA 1994, ss.3(6) and 32(3)).

Limited registration for retail service marks, long thought unregistrable in the UK, is now possible in Class 35. This change in UK practice follows OHIM's decision in *Giacomelli Sports Spa* (1999).

Definition of a trade mark

TMA 1994, s.1(1) provides that a trade mark is a *sign* capable of being *represented graphically*, capable of *distinguishing* goods or services of one undertaking from those of another undertaking. Each of the elements of this definition shall now be considered in turn:

(a) A "sign". The concept of a "sign" in UK trade mark law is very broad. Although there is no definition examples of signs provided in the Act include words, designs and shapes, but this is not an exhaustive list, hence colours and more unconventional marks such as sounds and smells should also be considered. A sign could be regarded as being *anything that conveys information* (*Phillips v. Remington* (1998)).

(b) Graphic representation. Signs must be represented graphically, *i.e.* be represented in such a way that third parties may determine and understand what the sign is. This requirement is normally satisfied by including an image of the mark in the trade mark application, but it has been suggested that provision of an image is not necessary provided that third parties can clearly identify the mark from the description (*Swizzels Matlow Ltd's Application* (1999)). It may be difficult, however, to graphically represent unconventional marks, but practice dictates, for example that *sound marks* are best represented by musical notation and for *shape marks* that it is best to submit photographs or line drawings of the shape from a number of different perspectives. Applications for *colour marks* (*i.e.* a specific shade of a colour, not an entire spectrum of a single colour) usually include a specimen of the relevant colour. However, colour marks may also be graphically represented by description, provided that description employs a known and recognised colour standard.

(c) Capable of distinguishing. Signs must be capable of distinguishing goods or services of one undertaking from those of another undertaking). Any sign that has the capacity to distinguish will satisfy this limited requirement (*AD2000 Trade Mark* (1996)).

ABSOLUTE GROUNDS FOR REFUSAL

Introduction

A sign will not be registered if it falls within one or more of the absolute grounds for refusing registration. Each absolute ground is considered below.

Signs not satisfying the s.1(1) requirements

Signs which do not meet the definition of "trade mark" provided in the TMA 1994 shall not be registered (TMA 1994, s.3(1)(a)), *i.e.* where the mark is not properly represented on the application form or is incapable of distinguishing, the application will fail.

The basic elements of *graphic representation* have already been considered above. It is important for a trade mark applicant not to make a mistake as to graphic representation, as the opportunity to correct such mistakes are limited (TMA 1994, s.39 prevents the correction of errors in a trade mark application that would substantially affect the identity of the trade mark). This is mitigated by the fact that it is Registry practice (in response to the decision in the *TY-NANT* (1999)) to examine marks for graphic representation before a filing date is allocated.

Scent marks, nevertheless, continue to cause particular difficulties for graphic representation and *John Lewis' Application (THE SCENT OF CINNAMON)* (2001) indicates a description of a scent is unlikely to be sufficiently precise. For CTM applications, OHIM appears to have adopted a more permissive approach than the UK Registry on this issue (*Vennootshap onder Firma Scenta Aromatic Marketing's Application (THE SCENT OF FRESHLY-CUT GRASS)* (1999)).

Signs must also be *capable of distinguishing* the goods or services of one undertaking from those of other undertakings. As noted above, this is not a high standard and, in effect, it will only bar those signs that are incapable of functioning as trade marks (*e.g.* the Philips shaver shape in *Philips Electronics v. Remington Consumer Products* (1999), a case discussed in relation to shape marks below, was held not to be distinctive in a trade mark sense and thus did not satisfy TMA 1994, s.3(1)(a)).

Proviso to TMA 1994, s.3(1)(b)(c) and (d)

Marks devoid of distinctive character or those consisting of exclusively descriptive or generic signs are prohibited *unless it can be shown that before the application was made, the mark has acquired a distinctive character as a result of the use made of it* (TMA 1994, s.3(1)). This proviso to TMA 1994, ss.3(1)(b)(c) and (d) means that there is no absolute prohibition as a matter of law on non-distinctive, descriptive and generic marks. As recognised in *British Sugar v. James Robertson (TREAT)* (1996)), such marks may be registered where they have become factually distinctive upon use despite the prohibitions stated in TMA 1994, s.3(1)(b)–(d).

This proviso does *not* apply to TMA 1994, s.3(1)(a) or any other absolute ground for refusal.

Marks devoid of distinctive character

TMA 1994, s.3(1)(b) prevents the registration of marks that are not, *prima facie*, distinctive. An example might include a surname common in the UK, such as WILSON (of course the proviso makes it possible for such a mark to *acquire* distinctiveness, after which it may be registerable).

In *British Sugar v. James Robertson (TREAT)* (1996), it was said that a mark is devoid of distinctive character where the sign cannot distinguish the applicant's goods or services without the public first being educated that it is a trade mark. The laudatory mark at issue in this case, TREAT for a syrup for pouring on ice cream and desserts, was therefore devoid of distinctive character. Such marks may, nevertheless, benefit from the TMA 1994, s.3(1) proviso. Therefore, trade marks will only fail under TMA 1994, s.3(1)(b) where they are not distinctive by nature and have not become distinctive by nurture (*AD2000 Trade Mark* (1996)).

Signs that are exclusively descriptive

For a sign to be open to objection under TMA 1994, s.3(1)(c), the trade mark must consist *exclusively* of a sign which may be used in trade to describe characteristics of the goods or services.

The sub-categories of TMA 1994, s.3(1)(c) are:

(i) Kind. Terms indicating kind or type that should be free for all traders to use, *e.g.* PERSONAL for computers, are not normally registrable.

(ii) Quality. Laudatory words, *e.g.* PERFECTION, are not usually registrable.

(iii) Quantity. The Trade Mark Registry gives the example that 454 would not be registrable for butter, as butter is frequently sold for domestic consumption in 454g (1lb) packs. Where numerical marks are not descriptive or otherwise objectionable, they may be registered.

(iv) Intended purpose. Generally, words referring to the purpose of goods or services are not registrable.

(v) Value. Signs pertaining to the value of goods or services are not normally registrable. *e.g.* BUY ONE, GET ONE FREE.

(vi) Geographical origin. Geographical names are not usually registrable unless used in specific circumstances. A fanciful use of a geographic name, *e.g.* EQUATOR for ice, would be permissible as here the name is unlikely to be taken as the origin of the goods.

(vii) Time of production of goods or the rendering of services. Typically, marks such as SAME DAY DELIVERY for courier services or AUTUMN 2002 for haute couture would not be registrable.

(viii) Other characteristics of goods or services. For example, a representations of the good or service would not be usually registrable.

Marks falling into any of these categories may still be registrable if they have become distinctive upon use (the TMA 1994, s.3(1) proviso).

In holding that BABY-DRY was registrable for disposable nappies (*Proctor & Gamble v. OHIM (BABY-DRY)* (2002)), the ECJ has implied that a wider category of descriptive marks than that hitherto considered, may be registrable. Consequently, the UK Registry may in future adopt a more generous approach to descriptive marks.

Signs that are exclusively generic

TMA 1994, s.3(1)(d) prohibits the registration of signs or indications that have become customary in the current language or in the bona fide and established practices of the trade. An example can be found in *JERYL LYNN Trade Mark* (1999), where an application for JERYL LYNN for vaccines was refused as the mark described a strain of vaccine and was not distinctive of the applicant.

As with TMA 1994, ss.3(1)(b) and (c), objections under this absolute ground for refusal may be overcome by the proviso, as in *Waterford Wedgewood v. David Nagli Ltd* (1998), where the registration of LISMORE was challenged. The defendant argued that LISMORE was the name of a pattern and style of cut glass and therefore the application should be barred under TMA 1994, s.3(1)(d). As the TMA 1994, s.3(1) proviso applied (there was evidence that the name had become distinctive of the applicant's glass), registration was allowed.

Unregisterable shapes

Traditionally in the UK, shapes were not registerable (see *Coca-Cola's Trade Mark Applications* (1986)). The TMA 1994 makes it clear that the shapes of goods and their packaging are now registerable (TMA 1994, s.1(1)), but TMA 1994, s.3(2) excludes certain shapes from registration. This is an area of trade mark law that has lacked clarity.

ECJ guidance on the registrability of shape marks has clarified matters to some extent. The UK Court of Appeal stayed proceedings in *Philips Electronics v. Remington Consumer Products* (1999) to allow a preliminary reference to the ECJ in a number of issues, including questions particular to shape marks and this decision has implications for the interpretation of TMA 1994 s.3(2) (see below). The facts of the *Philips* case itself may be briefly summarised as follows: Philips had long produced and sold a three-headed rotary shaver (the Philishave). When Remington introduced a rotary shaver of similar design (the DT55), Philips sued for infringement of a mark which was the face of the three-headed shaver.

The TMA 1994 provides that the following shapes are not registrable:

(a) Where the shape results from the nature of the goods themselves (TMA 1994, s.3(2)(a)). *Inherent shapes* cannot, therefore, be registered. In *Philips* (1999) the UK Court of Appeal considered that there would be no objection to Philips' three-headed shaver shape on this ground as electric shavers could take other forms.

(b) Where the shape of the goods is necessary to achieve a technical result (TMA 1994, s.3(2)(b)). *Functional shapes* cannot, therefore, be registered.

In *Philips* (1999) it was considered that the shaver shape *was* necessary to achieve a technical result, but the ECJ was, nevertheless, asked to adjudicate on the correct approach to functional shapes. Therefore, it now appears that the correct approach to s.3(2)(b) is to ask whether the essential aspects of the shape are necessary to achieve a technical result. Clearly, UK courts should avoid a narrow interpretation of s.3(2)(b) (is this the only shape that will achieve the technical result?). The ECJ also confirmed that the fact that there may be more than one shape that could achieve the same result is not relevant. Consequently, it appears that only shapes with significant non-functional aspects are registrable.

(c) Where the shape gives substantial value to the goods (TMA 1994, s.3(2)(c)). In *Phillips* (1999), the Court of Appeal suggested that a *valuable shape* in this context can be identified where the shape itself adds substantial value, *e.g.* the shape adds value via eye appeal or functional effectiveness. In contrast, shapes that are valuable because they are "good trade marks" would not fall foul of s.3(2)(c).

Marks likely to offend morals or deceive

A mark shall not be registered if it is contrary to public policy or accepted principles of morality (TMA 1994, s.3(3)(a)) or is of such a nature that it is likely to deceive the public (TMA 1994, s.3(3)(b)), for example as to the nature, quality or origin of the goods or services.

Relatively few marks are likely to be deemed contrary to public policy or morality as only the most shocking or outrageous terms should be denied registration under TMA 1994, s.3(3)(a) (*Ghazilian's Trade Mark Application* (2001)). Morality should be considered in the context of current thinking. Only where a substantial number of persons would be offended (such persons might, nevertheless, be in a minority in the community) should registration be refused; the context in which the allegedly offensive mark is to be used may be a factor in this assessment (*Ghazilian's Trade Mark Application* (2001)).

In *BOCM's Application (EUROLAMB)* (1997), EUROLAMB was considered to be deceptive (TMA 1994, s.3(3)(b)) if used in relation to non-sheep meat (when used in relation to sheep meat, it was descriptive). It is clear that the test of deception is objective and actual evidence of deception must be provided (*Kraft Jacobs Suchard Ltd's Application* (2001)).

Marks prohibited by UK or EC law

The registration of marks whose use would be illegal under UK or Community law is precluded by TMA 1994, s.3(1)(d).

Specially protected emblems

TMA 1994, s.4 provides details of marks that are considered to fall into the category of specially protected emblems, for example marks with Royal connotations and the Olympic symbol cannot be registered (TMA 1994, s.3(5)); marks containing such emblems may not be registered in the absence of consent.

Applications made in bad faith

There is no requirement that a mark need be used prior to the application for registration, but the applicant must have a *bona fide* intention to use the mark (TMA 1994, s.32(3)) and applications may be refused when they are made in bad faith (TMA 1994, s.3(6)). Therefore, so-called ghost applications would be caught by this section. An example of a ghost application under the old law was *Imperial Group v. Phillip Morris* (1982), where the applicant had registered the mark ghost mark NERIT so as to prevent others from using the word MERIT. Objections to overly wide registrations (where the applicant registers a mark for more goods or services than he intended to use the mark in) might also be made under TMA 1994, s.3(6); this possibility was considered in *Road Tech Computer Systems Ltd v. Unison Software* (1996).

More generally, dishonesty will fall into TMA 1994, s.3(6), but activities falling short of the standards of acceptable and reasonable commercial behavior will also be caught (*Gromax Plasticulture v. Don & Low (Nonwovens)* (1999)). Some deliberate action or behavior by the applicant is required (*Kraft Jacobs Suchard Ltd's Application* (2001)).

RELATIVE GROUNDS FOR REFUSAL

Introduction

The applicant must also overcome the relative grounds for refusing registration. These relate to conflict with earlier marks or earlier rights. The "earlier mark" (TMA 1994, s.6) might be a trade mark registered in the UK or under the Madrid Protocol. Alternatively it might be a CTM or a well—known mark (the latter are entitled to protection as *per* Article 6 of the Paris Convention for the Protection of Industrial Property 1883). There is provision for honest concurrent use in the TMA 1994 (TMA 1994, s.7). As it has been made clear that a trade mark application must be refused, irrespective of honest concurrent use, if the registered proprietor objects (*Road Tech Computer Systems v. Unison Software (ROAD-RUNNER)* (1997)), this provision is of limited value to the trade mark applicant. If the proprietor of the registered mark objects, honest concurrent use provides no defence and the Registry will apply the relevant sub-section of s.5

Any objections under the relative grounds for refusal can be overcome by obtaining the consent of the proprietor of the earlier mark (TMA 1994, s.5(5)).

Each relative ground for refusal is considered below.

Conflict with an earlier identical or similar mark for identical or similar goods or services

TMA 1994, s.5(1) provides the narrowest relative ground for refusing registration, a mark identical to an earlier trade mark and used for identical goods and services will not be registered. The requirement of "identical goods and services" is sufficiently broad to include cases where the applicant's mark is identical to only *some* of the goods and services for which the earlier mark is registered, but to constitute an "identical mark', a very high level of identity between the marks is required (*Origins Natural Resources v. Origin Clothing* (1995)).

The registration of similar marks for the same or similar goods or services is only prohibited where confusion on the part of the public is likely to arise (TMA 1994, s.5(2)). Specifically, what is prohibited is the registration of:

(i) Identical marks for similar goods or services (TMA 1994, s.5(2)(a)); or

(ii) Similar marks for identical/similar goods or services (TMA 1994, s.5(2)(b)). Where, because of the identity or similarity, there is a *likelihood of confusion* on the part of the public, which includes the *likelihood of association* with the earlier trade mark.

What constitutes "confusing similarity" has been considered at length by the ECJ (see *Sabel v. Puma* (1998) and *Canon v. Metro*

Goldwyn-Meyer (formerly Pathe (1999)). Confusion must be appreciated *globally*, taking into account all factors relevant the circumstances of the case. Factors to be taken into account in this global appreciation of confusion include:

(a) The *recognition* of the earlier trade mark on the market.
(b) The *association* that can be made between the registered mark and the sign.
(c) The *degree of similarity* between the mark and the sign and the goods or services, the degree of similarity must be considered in deciding whether the similarity is sufficient so as to lead to a likelihood of confusion.
  (i) Similarity of the marks in question should be judged upon consumer perception of the marks as a whole, bearing in mind their distinctive and dominant components. Similarity might be visual, phonetic or conceptual (*Sabel* (1998)). The more distinctive the earlier mark, the greater the likelihood of confusion (*Sabel* (1998)).
  (ii) Goods or services might be distinguished as to, for example, their nature, end users, cost, and the normal method of purchase or methods of use. Account may be taken of the distinctive character and repute of the earlier mark in deciding whether the similarity is sufficient so as to lead to a likelihood of confusion (*Canon* (1999)).

It has also been made clear that "likelihood of association" is not an alternative to "likelihood of confusion", but serves to define its scope. This means that if the public merely makes an association between two trade marks, this would not in itself be sufficient for concluding that there is a likelihood of confusion (*Sabel* (1998)); there is no likelihood of confusion where public would not believe that goods or services came from the same undertaking.

Conflict with a mark of repute

A mark that is identical or similar to an earlier mark will be refused registration in respect of *dissimilar* goods or services where the earlier mark is a mark of repute and the use of the later mark would, without due cause, take *unfair advantage* of or be *detrimental to* the reputed mark's distinctiveness or reputation

(TMA 1994, s.5(3)). Unlike TMA 1994, s.5(2), there is no requirement of confusion for this relative ground of refusal (see *Sabel* (1998) and *Canon* (1999)).

A mark of repute is a mark with a reputation in the UK (for CTM applications, it must be have a reputation in the EU). In deciding as to whether a trade mark has a reputation, the ECJ has provided some guidance (*General Motors Corp v. Yplon* (2000). Repute must be judged with reference to the general public or (if appropriate to the nature of the relevant product(s) or services(s)) to a specific section of the public, and the mark must be known to a *significant portion of that public*. Relevant indicators of the public's knowledge of the mark include the extent and duration of the trade mark's use, its market share and the extent to which it has been promoted.

In order for registration to be refused under s.5(3), use of the applicant's mark will have to take unfair advantage of or be detrimental to the reputed mark's distinctiveness or reputation. In *Oasis Stores Ltd's Application (EVEREADY)* (1998) it was said that merely being reminded of an opponent's mark did not itself amount to taking unfair advantage. The fact that the applicant did not benefit to any significant extent from the opponent's reputation and the wide divergence between the parties' goods was relevant, s.5(3) could not be intended to prevent the registration of *any mark* identical or similar to a mark of repute.

It is clear from infringement cases (the similar wording of s.5(3) and 10(3) mean that infringement cases can be relevant) that the concept of detriment includes dilution; dilution can occur via "blurring" where the distinctiveness of a mark is eroded or by the "tarnishing" of the mark's reputation (*Premier Brands v. Typhoon Europe* (2000)). It is also clear that the stronger a mark's distinctive character and reputation, the easier it is to establish detriment (*Premier Brands v. Typhoon Europe* (2000)).

Conflict with earlier rights

TMA 1994, s.5(4) provides that where a mark conflicts with earlier rights, including passing off, copyright and design rights, the mark will not be registered.

SURRENDER, REVOCATION. INVALIDITY, ACQUIESCENCE AND RECTIFICATION

(a) Surrender. It is possible to surrender one's trade mark with respect to some or all of the goods and services for which it is registered (TMA 1994, s.45).

(b) Marks may be revoked (removed from the Register) on three grounds (TMA 1994, s.45); non-use, because the mark has become generic, or because the mark has become deceptive.

(c) A mark will be invalid if it breaches any of the absolute grounds for refusing registration (TMA 1994, ss.47 and s.72).

(d) Where the proprietor of an earlier trade mark or other right is aware of the use of a mark subsequently registered in the UK and has, for a continuous period of five years, taken no action regarding that use the proprietor is said to have acquiesced. Where this is the case, the proprietor of the earlier mark or right cannot rely on his right in applying for a declaration of invalidity or in opposing the use of the later mark, unless it is being used in bad faith (TMA 1994, s.48).

(e) Any person with "a sufficient interest" can apply to rectify an error or omission in the Register. Such a rectification must not relate to matters that affect the validity of the trade mark (TMA 1994, s.64).

INFRINGEMENT

Introduction

The proprietor (and any exclusive licensee) has certain rights in his/her mark (TMA 1994, s.9(1)) which are infringed by certain forms of unauthorised use (as specified in TMA 1994, s.10) of the mark in the UK. These rights come into existence from the date of registration, which is the date of filing (TMA 1994, s.9(3)). A number of the infringement provisions are similar to the provisions that form the basis of the relative grounds for refusal (see above).

All infringing acts require the mark to be *used in the UK in the course of trade*. What constitutes "use" of a mark (see TMA ss.10(4) and 103(2)) has been the subject matter of some debate. For example, *obiter* comments in *1-800 Flowers Inc v. Phonenames Ltd* (2001) provide guidance as to what would constitute sufficient use of a mark on the internet. In this case it was felt that merely placing a mark on the internet from a non-UK location is insufficient to constitute use; the mark proprietor must actively promote their site to members of the UK public.

The acts that constitute trade mark infringement are discussed below.

Use of an identical sign for identical goods or services

Use, in the course of trade, of an identical sign in respect of identical goods or services constitutes trade mark infringement (TMA 1994, s.10(1)). This form of infringement mirrors TMA 1994 s.5(1), so please refer to that relative grounds for refusal, above.

Use of an identical or similar sign on identical or similar goods or services

Use, in the course of trade, of an identical sign on similar goods or services (TMA 1994, s.10(2)(a)), or a similar sign on identical or similar goods or services (TMA 1994, s.10(2)(b)) constitutes infringement where the public is likely to be confused as to the origin of the goods or services or is likely to assume that there is an association with the registered mark. This ground for infringement is the equivalent of TMA 1994, s.5(2). Please refer to the guidance provided for s.5(2), above.

Use of a mark similar to a mark of repute for dissimilar goods or services

Registered marks with a "reputation" are infringed if an identical or similar mark is used for non-similar goods or services, where the use takes unfair advantage of or is detrimental to, the distinctive character or repute of the registered mark (s.10(3) TMA 1994). This provision parallels that of s.5(3). Please refer to the reading and guidance provided for s.5(3), above.

Contributory infringement

TMA 1994, s.10(5) is known as the contributory infringement provision. This provision creates a form of secondary participation where a person who applies a trade mark to certain materials has actual or constructive knowledge that the use of the mark is not authorised. This provision extends infringement down the supply chain, but printers, publishers, manufacturers of packaging etc may avoid s.10(5) liability in practice via inserting suitable standard contractual terms into their agreements with their clients.

Defences to infringement

(a) Comparative advertising. Under the old law, comparative advertising (comparing X's goods with Y's or using X's mark as a way of praising Y's goods) constituted infringement. Now comparative advertising is allowed (TMA 1994, ss.10(6) and 11(1)(b)) under certain circumstances; in particular if the use is detrimental or takes unfair advantage of the distinctive character or repute of the trade mark, the use must be in accordance with the honest practices in industrial or commercial matters.

The TMA 1994 comparative advertising provisions were afforded a liberal interpretation in *British Airways PLC v. Ryanair Ltd* (2001). British Airways had brought an action for trade mark infringement against Ryanair for the publication of two Ryanair advertisements comparing Ryanair fares with those of British Airways. The action failed. In assessing as to whether a mark has been used in accordance with honest practices, the court should view the advertisement as a whole. Although misleading advertisements cannot be honest, on the facts, whilst the advertisement at issue may have caused offence it was not dishonest and the price comparisons were not significantly unfair.

(b) Use of another registered mark. Use of one registered mark, within the boundaries of the registration, does not infringe another registered mark (TMA 1994, s.11(1)).

(c) Use of own name or address. A person using his/her own name or address does not constitute infringement of a registered mark, provided that the person's use accords with appropriate honest practices (TMA 1994, s.11(2)(a)).

(d) Use of certain indications. The use of certain indications (*e.g.* the intended purpose of the goods or services or their geographical origin) will not constitute infringement where that use accords with appropriate honest practices (TMA 1994, s.11(2)(b)).

(e) The locality defence. Signs applicable to a particular locality whose use predates the registration of a mark may continue to be used in that locality (TMA 1994, s.11(3)). This provision enables a *local* user of a common law mark to continue that use if he would be protected in that locality by passing off.

(f) Exhaustion. Trade mark rights are exhausted once the proprietor has consented to the placing of goods bearing the mark on the market within the EEA (TMA 1994, s.12(1)). For example, once a brand owner consents to a consignment of their goods being marketed in France, trade mark rights cannot be used to prevent these goods from being resold in the UK (unless there are legitimate reasons for this, TMA 1994, s.12(2)). Goods resold in this way are known as "grey imports" or "parallel imports".

Remedies

Remedies are discussed in general in Chapter 2. The following remedies are available for trade mark infringement:

  (i) Damages (TMA 1994, s.14(2)).
 (ii) Account of profits (TMA 1994, s.14(2)).
(iii) Injunctions (TMA 1994, s.14(2)).
(iv) Erasure of the offending sign (TMA 1994, s.15).
 (v) Delivery up (TMA 1994, s.16).
(vi) Destruction or forfeiture of infringing goods (TMA 1994, s.19).

In addition:

 (i) In certain circumstances, threats to bring trade mark infringement proceedings can in themselves become actionable (TMA 1994, s.21).
(ii) Whilst there is no specific provision for the infringement of well-known marks not registered in the UK, the proprietor of such marks may restrain, by injunction, the use of identical or similar marks used in respect of identical or similar goods where confusion would result (TMA 1994, s.56).

CRIMINAL OFFENCES

There is both general and specific provision of criminal sanctions:

(a) Trade Descriptions Act 1968 and Consumer Protection Act 1987. In practice, various offences under these Acts may be applicable to trade marks.

(b) Offences under the Trade Mark Act 1994. Unauthorised use of a trade mark may constitute an offence (see TMA 1994, s.92). Other offences include falsification of the Register (TMA 1994, s.94) and falsely representing the mark as registered (TMA 1994, s.95)

6. PASSING OFF

INTRODUCTION

Passing off is a tort, historically developed from the tort of deceit (which had proved inadequate to protect producers that were suffering due to competitor's false assertions to be related to them). Passing off protects goodwill and as such it may be used in relation to marks, including unregistered marks (passing off is sometimes described as the law of unregistered trade marks). Many trade mark infringement cases also involve passing off issues and these two areas of law are closely related in practice.

The key criterion of a successful action in passing off is the presence of goodwill; it is goodwill, rather than the mark itself, that is protected in passing off.

PASSING OFF—WHICH TEST?

There are two possible tests for passing off:

(a) Lord Diplock identified five characteristics of a successful action in passing off in *Erven Warnink BV and Another v. J Townend & Sons (Hull) Ltd and Another (Advocaat)* (1980):

  (i) A misrepresentation.
  (ii) Made by a trader in the course of trade.
  (iii) To prospective customers of his or to ultimate customers of goods or services supplied by him.
  (iv) Which is calculated to injure the business or goodwill of another trader (in the sense that it is a reasonably foreseeable consequence); and

(v) This causes actual damage to a business or goodwill of the trader by whom an action is or will be brought.

(b) Lord Oliver reduced the *Advocaat* (1980) test to what is known as the "classic trinity" formulation in *Reckitt & Colman Products Ltd v. Borden Inc and Others (Jif Lemon)* (1990):

(i) The claimant must be able to demonstrate goodwill;
(ii) There must be a misrepresentation as to the goods or services offered by the defendant; and
(iii) Actual or likely damage.

Many UK cases follow the *Jif Lemon* (1990) formulation (*e.g.* *Consorzio del Prosciutto di Parma v. Marks & Spencer* (1991) and *BBC v. Talksport* (2001)). It also has the advantage of being simpler than the *Advocaat* (1980) test, therefore the *Jif Lemon* (1990) test is the formulation preferred in this work.

ELEMENTS OF PASSING OFF—GOODWILL

Definition of goodwill

Goodwill is a property right (as *per* Lord Diplock in *Star Industrial v. Yap Kwee Kor* (1976)). It is a somewhat amorphous concept, but has been most concisely defined by Lord Mac-Naughten as "the attractive force that brings in custom" (*The Commissioners of Inland Revenue v. Muller & Co* (1901)).

Goodwill is not the same as reputation (this distinction is considered in more detail in the context of territorial considerations, below) and reputation without goodwill is insufficient to support an action for passing off (*Anheuser-Busch v. Budejovicky Budvar Narodni Podnik (Budweiser)* (1984) and *Harrods v. Harrodian School* (1996)). The distinction between reputation and goodwill has also considered in *BBC v. Talksport* (2001). Here, the BBC was the only UK broadcaster entitled to broadcast live Euro 2000 football matches. The BBC objected to Talksport's advertising claim that its Euro 2000 coverage was "live" (Talksport had employed devices such as the addition of pre-recorded sound effects to its broadcasts, giving the false impression that its radio coverage constituted live broadcasts of the matches). The BBC failed in its claim for passing off—whilst the BBC had a *reputation* as a live broadcaster of sports, a reputation for this activity did not give rise to *protectable goodwill*.

The creation of goodwill

The concept of "trade" is key for establishing goodwill. "Trade" is not, however, restricted to commercial enterprises, non-profitmaking professional bodies have been able to benefit from passing off (*e.g. British Medical Association v. Marsh* (1931)), as have charities (*e.g. British Diabetic Association v. The Diabetic Society* (1996)).

Although "trade" has been interpreted generously in relation to non-profitmaking bodies, goodwill is seen as a legal property right associated with *business*.

The courts have considered it to be possible to create protectable goodwill within very brief periods of trading. For example, a mere three weeks was sufficient for goodwill to be established in the name MR CHIPPY for a mobile fish and chip van (*Stannard v. Reay* (1967)). As to whether goodwill is established, this is decided on a case by case basis; there are no set rules. In exceptional circumstances goodwill might be generated by pre-launch activity (*British Broadcasting Corporation v. Talbot Motors Co Ltd* (1981)).

The source of the goods or services is vital for establishing goodwill (see the discussion of territorial considerations, below).

It should be noted that goodwill does not necessarily cease when the business ceases trading (*Ad Lib Club v. Glanville* (1972)).

Distinctiveness

The claimant must demonstrate the presence of goodwill through signs distinctive of him/her in the public mind. The distinctive element might be a mark, logo, name, an "image" created through advertising, or, the get-up of a product. It is important to appreciate that passing off does not *directly* protect names, marks, get up or other indicia, but the *goodwill* in these.

It is naturally more difficult to build strong goodwill in, for example, a descriptive or generic mark. So, in *McCain International v. Country Fair Foods* (1981), the descriptive mark OVEN CHIPS was denied protection. Yet, establishing goodwill in a descriptive mark is not impossible, in *Antec International v. South Western Chicks (Warren) Ltd* (1997), it was established that the words FARM FLUID had come to be associated in the minds of farmers with Antec's product. Provided that those words were capable of being appropriated as a trade term, the claimant had shown that goodwill was established.

Get-up

There are particular difficulties as to the protection of get-up. Only get-up that is distinctive of the claimant as the source of the goods may benefit from the law of passing off. A high threshold has been set by the courts; merely novel or eye-catching packaging is not necessarily distinctive and therefore may not gain protection. Of the cases already considered, *Jif Lemon* (1990) and *McCain International v. Country Fair Foods (OVEN CHIPS)* (1981) concern get-up.

Goodwill—territorial and regional considerations

(a) Territorial considerations. It is possible for an overseas trader to have a *reputation* in the UK without actually trading in the UK. The question then arises, has *goodwill* been established in the UK? In *Anheuser-Busch v. Budejovicky Budvar Narodni Podnik (Budweiser)* (1984), the answer to this question was no. Here, the US manufacturers of Budweiser failed to demonstrate the necessary goodwill to sustain an action in passing off against a Czech company; American Budweiser was known in the UK, but was only available in US air bases on UK soil.

Only goodwill in the UK is relevant, and this may cause difficulties for the overseas claimant unless the business has managed to establish goodwill in the UK (*Jian Tools v. Roderick* (1995)). However, the foreign claimant's customers within the UK must be part of the general public (*Budweiser* (1984)).

(b) Regional considerations. Where a business may enjoy a local or national goodwill, the geographical area in which this is protected is, theoretically, limited accordingly. In practice, however, the courts have showed some reluctance to award an injunction which is subject to geographical restrictions (*e.g.* as in *Guardian Media Group v. Associated Newspapers* (unreported, 2000).

Shared goodwill

Where parties share goodwill in the same (distinct) product, goodwill attaches to the product and is shared by the manufacturers. In *Advocaat* (1980), manufacturers of Advocaat (a high quality liqueur made from brandewijn, eggs, yolks and sugar) were held to share goodwill, and, in *Tattinger SA v. Allbev Ltd* (1993) producers of champagne (which is precisely defined as sparkling wine produced by the méthode traditionale, from grapes produced in the Champagne region of France) were also held to share goodwill. The law in this area has been developed further by the Court of Appeal (*Chocosuisse Union des Fabricants Suisse de Chocolat v. Cadbury Ltd* (1999)).

ELEMENTS OF PASSING OFF—MISREPRESENTATION

The defendant must make a false representation, usually by using the signs that are distinctive of the claimant, which misleads the public. According to *Spalding v. Gamage* (1915), the misrepresentation can be innocent or fraudulent. The misrepresentation must, however, be material (*Miss World v. James St* (1981)).

The relevance of common field of activity

There is no rule in law stating that the parties must be in a common field of activity for passing off to occur *Irvine v. Talksport* (2002). What is needed, however, is an *association* between the defendant's and claimant's goods. Clearly, although these parties need not share a common field of activity, where this is the case it will be easier for the claimant to demonstrate that there has been a misrepresentation.

For example, in *Stringfellow v. McCain* (1984), Peter Stringfellow was unable to prevent STRINGFELLOW from being used in relation to chips. It has been suggested that the diversity between frozen chips and strip clubs was an important factor in this decision.

ELEMENTS OF PASSING OFF: DAMAGE

Actual or likely damage must result from the misrepresentation. Possible heads of damage include:

   (i) Direct loss of sales;
  (ii) Dilution;
 (iii) Inferiority of the defendant's goods;
 (iv) Injurious association;
  (v) Injury through constant confusion;
 (vi) Loss of licensing opportunity.

DEFENCES AND REMEDIES

Defences

  (i) Failure to establish the elements necessary for a passing off action;
 (ii) Acquiescence or delay;
(iii) Undeserving claimant;
 (iv) Use of own name;
  (v) Honest concurrent user.

Remedies

Remedies are discussed in general in Chapter 2. The following remedies are available for passing off:

  (i) Damages;
 (ii) Account of profits;
(iii) Delivery-up or destruction;
 (iv) Declaration;
  (v) Injunction.

INTERNET DOMAIN NAMES—PASSING OFF AND TRADE MARKS

Domain names, *e.g.* www.soton.ac.uk, may give rise to both passing off and trade mark issues. Domain names are signs which may be registered as trade marks, providing that they satisfy the usual criteria (see Chapter 5).

The leading case in this area is *British Telecommunications plc v. One in a Million Ltd* (1999). Here, One in a Million had registered a number of well-known trade marks with a view to making a profit by selling them on to the relevant brand owners and other third parties. This activity, known as cybersquatting, constituted a false representation to persons who consulted the domain name register that One in a Million was in some way connected or associated with the name registered, and this amounted to passing off. Also, even if TMA 1994, s.10(3) required the use as a trade mark, threats to infringe had been established. Registration of the domain names to exploit the marks' indications of origin, and the threatened disposal of the domain names, was unfair and harmful to the distinctive character and reputation of the trade marks.

The court also introduced the concept of *instrument of fraud*. The defendant's purpose in registering the domain names was to extract money from the owners of the goodwill in those names by the threat, whether express or implied, that the goodwill would be exploited by One in a Million (or by third parties); the domain names were therefore registered as an instruments of fraud.

PROBLEMATIC AREAS IN PASSING OFF

Endorsement or sponsorship

Some people may be in a position to exploit their personality or reputation in a particular field by endorsing goods or services. It follows, therefore, that the public may infer from the defendant's representation that the claimant is endorsing the defendant's product or services. It would seem that the claimant's endorsement must be valuable, that the public must infer endorsement from the defendant's representation and that the claimant is "in trade" (*Stringfellow v. McCain* (1984)).

Character merchandising

The image of a (usually fictional) character can be very valuable and can be used to sell a range of products and services. In practice, companies rely on a combination of trade marks and contract to protect official character merchandising. With the reform of registered designs, it is now also possible to utilise registered designs in this area (see Chapter 9, below). Historically in the UK, passing off has been unhelpful in character merchandising. The only successful case has been the interim decision in *Mirage Studios v. Counter-Feat (Teenage Mutant Ninja Turtles)* (1991).

Deception

Deception is not required as a necessary characteristic of a passing off action in the *Jif Lemon* (1990) formula. Nevertheless, deception of the public (which, confusingly, is often termed "confusion" in passing off cases) appears to be a key element of the successful passing off action in practice. For example, in *Morning Star v. Express Newspaper* (1979) it was said that even "the moron in a hurry," would not be deceived.

7. COPYRIGHT I—SUBSISTENCE OF COPYRIGHT

INTRODUCTION

What is copyright?

Copyright is a property right that subsists in certain works. It is a statutory right giving the copyright owner certain exclusive rights in relation to his/her work, such as the right to make copies of the work, to sell these copies to the public or the right to give a public performance of the work. A range of legislation is pertinent to copyright, with the main UK statute being the Copyright Designs and Patents Act 1988 (hereafter, CDPA 1988).

There are nine categories of copyright works:

"Authorial", "primary" or "LDMA" works (hereafter known as LDMA works):

   (i) Literary works;
  (ii) Dramatic works;
 (iii) Musical works;
  (iv) Artistic works.

"Entrepreneurial", "secondary" or "derivative" works (hereafter known as secondary works)

    (v) Sound recordings;
   (vi) Films;
  (vii) Broadcasts;
 (viii) Cable programmes;
   (ix) Typographical arrangement of published editions (the typography right).

Copyright comes into existence, or subsists, automatically where a *qualifying person* (qualification can also arise from the place of publication) creates a *work* that is *original* (or, for some works, not copied) and *tangible* (or fixed).

QUALIFICATION

Copyright will not subsist in a work unless:

(a) It has been created by a qualifying person (CDPA 1988, s.154).

(b) It was first published in a qualifying country, or transmitted from a qualifying country (CDPA 1988, ss.155 and 156).

(c) In the case of literary, dramatic and musical works, the work must fixed, that is reduced to a material form, in writing or otherwise (CDPA 1988, s.3(2)).

COPYRIGHT WORKS

Literary works

CDPA 1988, s.3(1) defines a literary work as being "any work written, spoken or sung, other than a dramatic or musical work." A novel, a poem or instructions on a cereal packet could equally fall into this category. Additionally, the concept of literary works extends to tables (*e.g.* a bus timetable), compilations (*e.g.* a directory or a CD collation of "The top 20 classical tunes"), and computer programs (including preparatory design material for computer programs). Databases (*e.g.* WESTLAW) are regarded as literary works (CDPA 1988, s.3A), but are different from "compilations" or "tables" (CDPA 1988, s.3(1)(a)).

In essence, any work that can be expressed in print, irrespective of its quality, will be a literary work (*University of London Press v. University Tutorial Press* (1916)).

Dramatic works

CDPA 1988, s.3(1) defines "dramatic work" as including works of dance or mime. In *Norowzian v. Arks* (No. 2) (1999) it was stated that these terms should be given their natural and ordinary meaning; the implication being that dramatic works are works of *action*. The court also recognised in this case that films may be protected as dramatic works, either as dramatic works in themselves and/or as a recording of a dramatic work.

Musical works

A musical work is a work consisting exclusively of musical notes, any words or actions intended to be sung, spoken or performed with the notes are excluded (CDPA 1988, s.3(1)(a)).

This means that whilst the melody of a popular song would constitute a musical work, the lyrics of the song would be a literary work.

Artistic works

A wide-ranging definition of "artistic work" is provided by CDPA 1988, s.4. Works of architecture (buildings or models of buildings) are included but focus is usually placed on the remaining artistic works. These fall into two categories:

(a) Works protected *irrespective of their artistic merit* (CDPA 1988, s.4(1)(a)). The inevitably difficult questions concerning artistic judgement (*Hi-Tech Autoparts Ltd v. Towergate Two Ltd (No. 1)* (2002)) can be ignored for the following artistic works:

   (i) Graphic works, *i.e.* paintings, drawings, diagrams, maps, charts, plans, engravings, etchings, lithographs, woodcuts or similar works.

     It should be noted that as there is no requirement of artistic merit, functional items may be graphic works. Further, items used in the production of such works may themselves be protected, for example many graphic works are produced from engravings which may themselves be copyright works. This is an area where design law and copyright overlap, see Chapter 9 for further information.

   (ii) Photographs.

   (iii) Sculptures. The protection of functional objects, such as a cast, is, again, problematic here. Famously in a New Zealand case, *Wham-O Manufacturing Co v. Lincoln Industries Ltd* (1985) a wooden model of a Frisbee was held to be a sculpture. The modern UK position is almost certainly more restrictive, as objects will not now be protected as sculptures where they are not made for the purposes of sculpture (*J&S Davis (Holdings) Ltd v. Wright Health Group* (1988)).

   (iv) Collages. Collages are artistic or functional visual arrangements produced via affixing two or more items together. Intrinsically ephemeral arrangements (for example, the composition of a photograph as in *Creation Records Ltd v. News Group Newspapers Ltd* (1997)) are not collages.

(b) Artistic works *required to be of a certain quality* (CDPA 1988, s.4(1)(c)), *i.e.* works of artistic craftsmanship. Few works can meet the standards of artistic craftsmanship, as they must be *both* be of artistic quality and be the result of craftsmanship (*George Hensher Ltd v. Restawhile* (1976)). These principles were further developed into a two-part test for artistic craftsmanship in *Merlet v. Mothercare plc* (1986), first, did the creation of the work involve craftsmanship in the sense that skill and pride was invested in its manufacture? Second, does the work have aesthetic appeal, and, did an artist create it?

Sound recordings

A sound recording is a reproducible recording of either:
   (i) Sounds where there is no underlying copyright work (*e.g.* birdsong, the sound of waves) (CDPA 1988, s.5A(1)(a); or
  (ii) A recording of the whole or any part of a literary, dramatic or musical work (CDPA 1988, s.5A(1)(b)).

The format of the recording (vinyl record, audio or videotape, DVD, etc.) is irrelevant.

Film

CDPA 1988, s.5B(1) provides that a film is a reproducible recording of a moving image on any medium (*e.g.* celluloid or digital recordings). It is the recording itself that is protected, rather than the subject matter that has been recorded, but it should be borne in mind that a film may also be protected as a dramatic work. Film soundtracks are taken to be part of the film itself (CDPA 1988, s.5B(2)).

Broadcasts

Copyright subsists in sounds and visual images that are broadcast (CDPA 1988, s.6(1)), a broadcast being defined as as a transmission by wireless telegraphy of visual images, sounds or other information. The definition of "broadcast" therefore encompasses radio and television broadcasts and both terrestrial and satellite broadcasting.

Cable programmes

The transmission of an item that forms part of a cable programme service will create separate works that are capable of protection as cable programmes (CDPA 1988, s.7). A cable programme service is defined as a service consisting wholly or mainly in sending visual images, sounds or other information via a telecommunications system which may utilise wires or microwave transmission. Items sent via wireless telegraphy are specifically excluded as they are already protected as broadcasts. This means that as well as obvious candidates such as subscription cable television services, a website on the Internet may be a cable programme service (*The Shetland Times v. Wills* (1997)).

The typography right

CDPA 1988, s.8 affords protection to the typography, that is the layout, of published editions of literary, dramatic and musical works (although these underlying works need not themselves be the subject of copyright protection). The leading authority on typographical arrangement copyright is *Newspaper Licensing Agency Ltd v. Marks & Spencer plc* (2001).

Copyright works: the idea/expression dichotomy

There is no copyright in ideas; copyright subsists in the *tangible expression* of ideas, not in the ideas themselves. In America this is referred to as the idea/expression dichotomy. This principle can be helpful but should not be taken too literally, as whilst it is clear that mere ideas cannot be protected by copyright (*e.g.* catchphrases and other features of a game show in *Green v. New Zealand Broadcasting Corp* (1989) or editing techniques and styles in *Norowzian v. Arks (No. 2)* (1999)), the following points should be noted:

(i) What might be termed "highly developed ideas", *e.g.* an early draft of a textbook, would be protected by copyright, as are preparatory design material for computer programs (CDPA 1988, s.3(1)(c)); and

(ii) Copyright cannot be circumvented by selectively altering the expression of a copyright work in the process of reproducing it (*i.e.* infringement is not limited to an exact reproduction of how the work was expressed. As noted in Chapter 8, infringement will be found were there is a *substantial taking* of a copyright work).

GINALITY

CDPA 1988, s.1 requires that literary, dramatic, musical and artistic works be "original". The originality requirement only applies to LDMA works, there is no such requirement for the secondary copyright works, although it is clear that no copyright will subsist in secondary copyright works that merely reproduce existing secondary works (*e.g.* see CDPA 1988, s.5A(2)).

LDMA works must be original in the sense that they originate with the author (*University of London Press v. University Tutorial Press* (1916)). This is a minimal qualitative requirement: original works need not be inventive or original and a wide range of work have been held to be original, from coupons for football pools (*Ladbrokes v. William Hill* (1964) to a compilation of broadcasting programmes (*Independent Television Publications Ltd and the BBC v. Time Out Ltd* (1984)).

Expending skill and judgement in creating an LDMA work usually suffices to deem the work original. Mere copying cannot confer originality (*Interlego AG v. Tyco* (1989)), the pre-existing work must be developed or embellished in some way for copyright to subsist in the new work (although such activity may still constitute copyright infringement).

Alternatively, the mere expenditure of effort or labour (the so-called "sweat of the brow" test for originality) has some-times been said to be sufficient to confer originality, but in practice some minimum element of skill or judgement is also usually required. Certainly in the past, "sweat of the brow" has been deemed insufficient, for example in *Cramp v. Smythson* (1944) it was held that the generic nature of com-monplace diary material left no room for judgement in selec-tion and arrangement, therefore the resultant works were not original. Originality has also been held to require more than "competent draftsmanship" (*Interlego v. Tyco* (1988)). Com-monly, databases and computer programs were the subject matter of "sweat of the brow" concerns. This low test for originality would seem less relevant now, given that both databases and computer programs are now subject to a higher statutory standard of originality (see below), as well as the fact that databases may also be protected by the *sui generis* database right (see Chapter 8).

Higher standards of originality: computer programs and databases

As a result of two European Directives, namely the Directive on the legal protection of databases (Directive 96/9/EC) and the Computer Directive (Directive 91/250/EEC), both computer programs and databases must be original in the sense that they are the author's own intellectual creation. This is a higher standard of originality than that of "skill, labour and judgement". The higher standard of originality is made explicit in the CDPA 1988, for databases (CDPA 1988, s.3A(2)) but, interestingly, no equivalent provision was introduced for computer programs.

Originality and the *de minimis* principle

Does copyright subsist in very short works? *Exxon Corporation v. Exxon Ind* (1982), where the invented word "Exxon" was denied copyright protection, is often cited to support the proposition that a *de minimis* principle applies in copyright law, *i.e.* that some things are too small to be deemed copyright works. However, the authority for this is not entirely clear; decisions in this area often seem motivated by policy considerations rather than the brevity of the alleged copyright work. For example, the fact that "Exxon" would be more appropriately protected by other intellectual property rights, such as trade mark law or passing off may have been an underlying consideration in the decision in *Exxon Corporation v. Exxon Ind* (1982)). In reality, the concept of originality (as well as other established copyright notions such as the idea/expression dichotomy) is more than equal to the task of objecting to truly trivial works—a separate *de minimis* principle may not be necessary and may be actively confusing.

FIXATION AND TANGIBILITY

Copyright does not subsist in literary, dramatic or musical works until they are recorded in writing or otherwise (CDPA 1988, s.3(2)). This pragmatic requirement is known as "fixation". Usually such works will be fixed by the author, but fixation by a third party (with or without the author's permission) is also possible (CDPA 1988, s.3(3)).

Other copyright works are not subject to the fixation requirement. This is usually unproblematic as films, sound recordings, broadcasts, cable programs and typography are inherently tangible works. Problems may arise with artistic works where their form is transitory or otherwise lack permanence. Whilst there is no statutory requirement of fixation for artistic works, the courts do in fact require artistic works to be tangible and permanent (see *Merchandising Corp of America v. Harpbond* (1983) and *Komesaroff v. Mickle* (1988)).

OWNERSHIP OF COPYRIGHT AND THE EMPLOYEE AUTHOR

The basic rule is that the first owner of copyright in a work is the person who created the work, the author, (CDPA 1988, s.11(1)). A major exception to this rule is CDPA 1988, s.11(2), which provides that where a person creates an LDMA work in the course of employment, the employer is the first owner of any copyright in the work, subject to an agreement to the contrary (such an agreement could be written, oral or implied from conduct). There are also special provisions for Crown use, Parliamentary copyright and copyright for certain international organisations (CDPA 1988, s.11(3)).

Who is the author?

The author is the person who creates the work (CDPA 1988, s.9(1)), the person whose skill, labour and effort brings the work into existence. It therefore follows, for example, that the person who writes a literary work is usually the author of that work. However if he/she were taking dictation, the speaker would be the author, not the writer, as the writer in dictation is merely acting as an amanuensis (*Donoghue v. Allied Newspapers* (1938), but *CF Walter v. Lane* (1900)). Identifying the author is usually a straightforward task and the table below summarises the standard authorship position:

COPYRIGHT	PERSON(S) USUALLY TAKEN TO BE THE AUTHOR(S)
Literary work	The writer (CDPA 1988, s.9(1))
Dramatic work	The writer (CDPA 1988, s.9(1))

COPYRIGHT	PERSON(S) USUALLY TAKEN TO BE THE AUTHOR(S)
Musical work	The composer (CDPA 1988, s.9(1))
Artistic work	The artist (CDPA 1988, s.9(1))
Computer generated LDMA works	The person operating the computer (CDPA 1988, s.9(3))
Sound recordings	The producer (CDPA 1988, s.9(2)(aa)
Films	The producer and principal director (CDPA 1988, s.9(2)(ab)
Broadcasts	The broadcaster (CDPA 1988, s.9(2)(b))
Cable programmes	The cable programme service provider (CDPA 1988, s.9(2)(c))
Typography right	The publisher (CDPA 1988, s.9(2)(d)).
Any work where the identity of the author is unknown	A work of unknown authorship (CDPA 1988, s.9(4) and (5))

Joint authorship

Complications arise where more than one person is involved in the creation of a work. Determining whether a person's contribution is sufficient for them to be deemed an author and whether joint authorship or co-authorship is present, demands careful consideration of the facts. A person who suggests a subject to a poet is not the author of the resultant poem (*e.g.* see *Tate v. Thomas* (1921)). Merely supplying ideas is insufficient for joint authorship (*Wiseman v. George Weidenfeld and Nicholson Ltd and Donaldson* (1985)), an integral role in the expression of those ideas is required, as in *Cala Homes v. Alfred McAlpine Homes* (1995).

Joint authorship (CDPA 1988, s.10(1)) arises when the efforts of two or more authors are indistinguishable (*e.g. Cala Homes v. Alfred McAlpine Homes* (1995)).

Ownership and employees

Where LDMA works or films are created by employees, the first owner of copyright in these works will vest in the employer when (CDPA 1988, s.11(2)):

(a) The work was created by an employee (see *Stephenson Jordan & Harrison v. MacDonald* (1952)).
(b) It was created during the course of employment (see *Noah v. Shuba* (1991)).
(c) There is no agreement to the contrary.

The distinction between a contract of service and a contract for services is important for identifying who is an employee. Persons employed as consultants or persons commissioned to produce copyright works are not employees and therefore not subject to CDPA 1988, s.11(2), so the position as to ownership of copyright must thus be made clear via contract. Any transfer of copyright must be in signed writing (CDPA 1988, s.90(3)). It is possible to deal in future copyrights (CDPA 1988, s.91), but again, assignment must be in signed writing (CDPA 1988, s.91(1)).

---

8. COPYRIGHT II—INFRINGEMENT, REMEDIES AND NEIGHBOURING RIGHTS

INTRODUCTION TO INFRINGEMENT

Infringement may take two forms, *primary* infringement and *secondary* infringement. Primary infringement occurs where restricted acts are carried out without the permission of the copyright owner. Secondary infringement is concerned with large-scale infringements taking place with actual or constructive knowledge, *i.e.* forms of piracy. Nevertheless, most secondary infringements will be based on an earlier primary infringement; for example, dealing in infringing copies will usually be based on an earlier infringement of the primary reproduction rights.

The restricted acts

The copyright owner has the exclusive right to do certain restricted acts in relation to his/her copyright work. *Primary infringement* occurs where any person (directly or indirectly) carries out, or proports to authorise another to carry out, any of these restricted acts, without the permission of the copyright owner, in relation to the whole or a substantial part of the copyright work (CDPA 1988, s.16(2)). The restricted acts are (CDPA 1988, s.16(1)):

(a) To copy the work (known as the reproduction right);
(b) To issue copies of the work to the public (known as the distribution right);
(c) To rent or lend the work to the public (known as the rental and lending rights);
(d) To perform, show or play the work in public (known as the public performance right);
(e) To broadcast the work or include it in a cable programme service (known as the broadcasting and cable rights);
(f) To make an adaptation of the work, or to do any of the above acts in relation to an adaptation of the work (known as the adaptation right).

Secondary infringement (CDPA 1988, ss.22–26) usually occurs where there is commercial use of a copyright work; it concerns the commission of certain acts, without the permission of the copyright owner, with respect to infringing copies (CDPA 1988, s.27) or the means of producing infringing copies. Unlike primary infringement, secondary infringement requires that the infringer knows or has reason to believe that he/she is dealing with infringing copies of a work. Secondary infringement concerns:

(a) Importing an infringing copy;
(b) Possessing an infringing copy;
(c) Selling, exhibiting or distributing an infringing copy;
(d) Dealing with items that are used for the making of infringing copies of specific works;

(e) Permitting premises to be used for an infringing performance or providing apparatus for such performances.

PRIMARY INFRINGEMENT

Taking the whole or a substantial part of a copyright work

This is a key element of primary infringement. First, the claimant's copyright work must be the *source* of the allegedly infringing work (*Francis Day & Hunter v. Bron* (1963)). This causal connection may be indirect (*Plix Products v. Winstone* (1986)) or even subconscious, but if the allegedly infringing work was created independently it will not infringe (*Francis Day & Hunter v. Bron* (1963)).

Secondly, the *extent* of the taking is important. When the whole of a work has been taken for the purposes of carrying out a restricted act (*e.g.* for copying), infringement is straightforward. More difficult is where part of the claimant's copyright work is taken for these purposes, as it then must be decided whether the taking is substantial.

The CDPA 1988, provides no definition of "substantial", but some guidance can be found in the case law. It is clear that one assesses *both* the *quality* and the *quantity* of the taking from the claimant's work in deciding whether there has been a substantial taking (*Ladbroke Football Ltd v. William Hill (Football) Ltd* (1964)). Some attempts have been made to suggest a percentage test (*i.e.* "where x per cent of the claimant's work is taken by the defendant, then that is a substantial taking"), but this is unhelpful and ignores the qualitative aspect of the approach to this issue. Factors that do seem to influence the decisions on this issue include:

(i) The distinctiveness of the portion taken. For example, in *Hawkes v. Paramount Films* (1934), twenty-eight bars of a song amounted to a substantial taking of the underlying musical work, but these bars amounted to a highly recognisable portion of that song.

(ii) The nature of the copyright work appears to have some relevance, as the dividing line between idea and expression appears to be intrinsically clearer in some copyright works than for others. For example, when a melody brings to mind that of an earlier song, this is often because it is substantially the same as that of the earlier song. As taking relatively small portions of musical works can infringe (*e.g. Hawkes v. Paramount Films* (1934)), this may well constitute infringement. In contrast, establishing infringement may be more problematic in relation to artistic works. Two artistic works may share recognisable *concepts*, but as there is much scope to express them in a different way this may not be enough to constitute infringement (see *e.g. Bauman v. Fussell* (1953)).

(iii) The timing of the taking. In most cases, a substantial portion of a copyright work will be taken at a single point in time and taking will be a single event. It is more difficult to establish that a number of small takings (individually insubstantial, but significant when added up) over a period of time constitutes copyright infringement (*Electronic Techniques v. Critchley* (1997)).

Interesting issues may also be found in relation to the following activities:

(i) Sampling. In the music industry, the process of taking a small but recognisable part of a recording and repeating it, together with other material, to form a new recording may result in a new copyright work. However, where substantial portions of other copyright works have been taken, this will still constitute infringement.

(ii) Computer programs. A computer program might be protected by patent law (see Chapter 2) and/or by copyright as an original literary work. Where the whole or a substantial part of an original program's code is copied, a finding of infringement is usually straightforward (*e.g. Ibcos v. Barclay* (1994)). More problematic is where the structure, function or appearance of a program is taken; such issues are considered in *Ibcos v. Barclay* (1994) and *Cantor Fitzgerald v. Tradition* (2000).

Authorising infringement

Authorising any of the restricted acts also constitutes primary infringement (CDPA 1988, s.16(2)), *e.g. MCA Records v. Charly* (2002). The main principles of authorising infringement are set out in *CBS v. Amstrad* (1988).

Infringement of the reproduction right

Reproducing (copying) the whole or a substantial part of an LDMA work in any material form, including electronic storage, constitutes infringement (CDPA 1988, s.17(2)). This would include taking a photograph of a painting or making a drawing of a sculpture (CDPA 1988, s.17(3)). What is not included is use of design documents or models recording a copyright work (other than an artistic work) to produce an article (CDPA 1988, s.51(1)). It is also not an infringement to make a three-dimensional work from written instructions (*e.g. Foley v. Elliot* (1982)). There are also specific provisions relating to secondary works (CDPA 1988, ss.1794) and (5)).

Infringement of the distribution right

The copyright owner has the exclusive right of first distribution, within the EEA, of copies of the work, subject to the doctrine of exhaustion (CDPA 1988, s.18). See *Infabrics v. Jaytex* (1982).

Infringement of the rental and lending rights

This applies to LDMA works (other than works of architecture or applied art), films and sound recordings (CDPA 1988, s.18A). It is an infringement to rent or lend copies of such works without the permission of the copyright owner.

Infringement of the public performance right

CDPA 1988, s.19 provides that any work, other than an artistic work, is infringed by performance in public, where the copyright owner has not given permission. A performance could be visual and/or acoustic and be "live" and/or recorded (*e.g.* playing a recorded song). The courts are clear that performances in non-domestic contexts constitute performances in public, *e.g.* performances in a factory constituted a public performance in *Ernest Turner v. PRS* (1943). However, performances to sizeable or paying audiences in a semi-domestic scenario are more problematic. See *Jennings v. Stephens* (1936) and *PRS v. Harlequin* (1979).

Infringement of the broadcasting and cable rights

Broadcasting a work or including it in a cable programme, without the permission of the copyright owner, constitutes infringement (CDPA 1988, s.20).

Infringement of the adaptation right

Literary, dramatic and musical works are infringed where they are adapted (CDPA 1988, 21(3)). This includes translation and transcribing, such as a novel being turned into a play, in certain circumstances (CDPA 1988, s.21). It is clear that this extends to adaptation of computer programs (CDPA 1988, s.21(3)(ab)) and that many adaptations may also involve copying.

SECONDARY INFRINGEMENT

Where making an article involved copyright infringement, that article will be an "infringing copy"—commercial dealings in such copies often constitutes secondary infringement. Secondary infringement occurs where a person, without the license of the owner and with actual or constructive knowledge (this is assessed objectively), does any of the following:

  (i) Imports an infringing copy (CDPA 1988, s.22);
 (ii) Possesses an infringing copy (CDPA 1988, s.23);
(iii) Sells, exhibits or distributes an infringing copy (CDPA 1988, s.23);
(iv) Deals with items that are used for the making of infringing copies of specific works (CDPA 1988, s.24);
 (v) Permits premises to be used for an infringing performance (CDPA 1988, s.25); or provides apparatus for such performances (CDPA 1988, s.26).

PERMITTED ACTS

CDPA 1988, s.16(4) provides that the restricted acts are themselves subject to permitted acts (CDPA 1988, ss.28–76) and the copyright licensing provisions (CDPA 1988, s.116 onwards). Discussion of the latter is beyond the scope of this work. Activities falling within the permitted acts will not infringe copyright. There are a large number of permitted acts and a simplified version of the main permitted acts is given in the following table:

PERMITTED ACT	OUTLINE OF SCOPE OF PERMITTED ACT
Fair dealing for the purposes of **research and private study** (CDPA 1988, s.29)	Applies to LDMA works and to the typography right. The reproduction of such works for commercial purposes falls outside this provision, *e.g. Sillitoe v. McGraw-Hill* (1983). There is a specific provision for databases in s.21(1A).
Fair dealing for the purposes of **criticism or review** (CDPA 1988, s.30(1))	Applies to all copyright works, but a sufficient acknowledgement of the title and author of the copyright work is required. See *Pro Sieben v. Carlton* (1999).
Fair dealing for the purposes of **reporting current events** (CDPA 1988, s.30(2))	Applies to all copyright works except photographs. The use must relate to a current event, even where older materials are used. Acknowledgement is required unless it is a sound recording, film, broadcast or cable programme. See *BBC v. BSB* (1992) and *Newspaper Licensing Agency Ltd v. Marks & Spencer plc* (2001).
Incidental inclusion (CDPA 1988, s.31)	Incidental inclusion of copyright material in an artistic work, sound recording, film, broadcast or cable programme will not infringe copyright. However, as *per* s.31(3), where musical works are deliberately included, this will still constitute infringement.

PERMITTED ACT	OUTLINE OF SCOPE OF PERMITTED ACT
The **educational exceptions** (CDPA 1988, ss.32–36A)	Various narrow exceptions for educational institutions.
The **library and archive exemptions** (CDPA 1988, s.37–44)	Various narrow exceptions for libraries and archives.
Making **back up copies** of computer programs (CDPA 1988, s.50A),	This will not infringe when carried out by a lawful user for a permitted purpose.
Decompilation of a computer program for the purposes of achieving interoperability (CDPA 1988, s.50B)	This will not infringe where the decompilation is for the purposes of achieving interoperability.
The **spoken word exception** (CDPA 1988, s.58)	Where the speaker withholds permission use of records of spoken words for certain purposes is permitted where certain requirements are satisfied.
Recording transmissions for **time shifting** (CDPA 1988, s.70)	Recording a broadcast or cable programme, *e.g.* on a video or a cassette tape, is permitted for private and domestic use where it is for the purposes of time shifting.
The **public interest defence** (CDPA 1988, s.171(3))	Applies to all copyright works. The courts may refuse to enforce copyright, either entirely or in part, where there is a public interest in publication or any other rule of law is relevant, *e.g.* non-derogation from grant in *British Leyland v. Armstrong* (1986). See "Copyright—the impact of the Human Rights Act 1998", below.

REMEDIES

Remedies are discussed in general in Chapter 2. The following remedies are available for copyright infringement:

(i) Damages (CDPA 1988, s.96), but innocent infringement does not give rise to a right to damages (CDPA 1988, s.97). However, additional damages (CDPA 1988, s.97(2)) may be available. These are calculated having regard to all the circumstances, including the flagrancy of the breach and any benefit accruing to the defendant from the infringement.

(ii) Injunctions (CDPA 1988, s.96).

(iii) Account of profits (CDPA 1988, s.96).

(iv) Seizure of infringing copies (CDPA 1988, s.100).

(v) Delivery up of infringing copies and articles specifically designed or adapted for the making copies (CDPA 1988, s.99).

(vi) Criminal offences (CDPA 1988, ss.107–108).

Moral rights (discussed below) are protected as a breach of statutory duty (CDPA 1988, s.103(1)). Damages are available and injunctions may be obtained, but, as *per* CDPA 1988, s.103(2), injunctions may be unavailable in relation to the integrity right where the defendant has made a disclaimer disassociating the author from the treatment of the work at issue.

COPYRIGHT—THE IMPACT OF THE HUMAN RIGHTS ACT 1988

An individual's right to privacy and the right to freedom of expression (these are considered in Chapter 4, above) may be relevant to the enforcement of copyright. For example, they may be relevant to the public interest defence or relate to issues of fair dealing. *Hyde Park v. Yelland* (2000) and *Paddy Ashdown MP v. Telegraph Group Ltd* (2001) are amongst the cases that should be considered here.

MORAL RIGHTS

These are personal rights (CDPA 1988, s.94) conferred upon the author of primary copyright works and the directors of films and are quite separate from the economic interests in the work.

There are four moral rights—the right of paternity, the right to integrity, the right to object to false attribution and the right to privacy in photographs and films. These are very specific rights and may be waived by the author (CDPA 1988, s.87).

Paternity

Authors of LDMA works and directors of films have the right to be identified as such, in certain situations (CDPA 1988, s.77). In order to benefit, the author/director must assert his/her right (CDPA 1988, ss.77(1) and 78) and there are a variety of exceptions (CDPA 1988, s.79).

Integrity

CDPA 1988, ss.80–83 concern the right of authors of LDMA works and directors of films to object to the derogatory treatment of their work: that is, that the work has been added to, altered to deleted (CDPA 1988, s.80(2)) in such a way to amount to a distortion, multilation or otherwise prejudicial treatment. CDPA 1988, s.81 sets out the exceptions to infringement. Cases such as *Tidy v. Trustees of the Natural History Museum* illustrate that it can be difficult to succeed with a claim of breach of the integrity right.

False attribution

Any person has the right for LDMA works and films not to be incorrectly attributed to him/her (CDPA 1988, ss.84–86). The attribution may be express, but it can also be implied. See, for example, *Clark v. Associated Newspapers* (1998).

Privacy in photos and films

The commissioner of photographs or a film has certain rights of privacy in relation to these where they are commissioned for private purposes (CDPA 1988, s.85), *e.g. Mail Newspapers v. Express Newspapers* (1987).

THE DURATION OF COPYRIGHT AND NEIGHBOURING RIGHTS

The rules governing duration of copyright are complicated by a number of factors, principally the number of copyright works (see Chapter 7) and the fact that the rules for many such works were changed by the Term Directive (Directive 93/98/EEC). The implementation of the Directive meant that the term of many existing copyright works were extended and some works in which copyright had previously lapsed, were revived. The following table is a simplified guide to the main rules on copyright duration and also the duration of the neighbouring rights (the latter are introduced below):

RIGHT	DURATION
Copyright in **LDMA works** (CDPA 1988, s.12(2))	70 years from the end of the calendar year in which the author dies (life plus 70 years).
Copyright in **works of joint authorship** (CDPA 1988, s.12(8))	70 years after the death of the last surviving author.
Copyright in **LDMA works of unknown authorship** (CDPA 1988, ss.12(3)–(5))	70 years from the date it was made, or, if during that period the work was made available to the public, 70 years from when it was made so available. If the authors name is discovered before this 70 year period expires and the author is still alive, then the term is extended to the normal copyright period of life plus 70 years.
Copyright in **computer generated LDMA works** (CDPA 1988, s.12(7))	50 years from the end of the year in which the work was made.
Copyright in **films** (CDPA 1988, s.13B)	70 years from the end of the calendar year in which the last of the following persons dies:

RIGHT	DURATION
	• the principal director of the film • the author of the film screenplay • the dialogue author, or • the film music composer. If the identity of these persons is unknown, then protection is for 70 years from the year in which the film was made, but where the film is made available to the public within this period, it becomes 70 years from the end of the year in which the film was made available to the public.
Copyright in **sound recordings** (CDPA 1988, s.13A)	50 years from the making of the sound recording, or, if released during that period, 50 years from its release.
Copyright in **broadcasts** and **cable programs** (CDPA 1988, s.14)	50 years from the making of the broadcast or from when the programme was first included in a cable program.
Copyright in the **typographical arrangement of published editions** (CDPA 1988, s.15)	25 years from the year of first publication.
Crown Copyright (CDPA 1988, s.163(3) in LDMA works	125 years from the year in which it was made or 50 years from the date it was commercially published, whichever is the lower.
Parliamentary Copyright (CDPA 1988, s.165(3))	50 years from the year in which the work was made.

RIGHT	DURATION
Moral rights (CDPA 1988, s.86)	The integrity and paternity rights last for as long as copyright. The right to object to false attribution endures for the author's lifetime plus 20 years.
Performers rights (CDPA 1988, s.191(2))	50 years from the performance or the release of the recording of the performance.
Sui generis **database right**	15 years from the making of the database.
Public lending right	This lasts as long as the underlying copyright

NEIGHBOURING RIGHTS

This is a general term taken to refer to rights outside copyright law, but related to it, including performers" rights, the *sui generis* database right and the public lending right. Each is very briefly described below.

Performers' rights

There are a number of rights intended to protect the performers of dramatic works, musical works, some literary works and "variety acts" (CDPA 1988, s.180(2)):

   (i) The right to authorise the recording of a live performance made for various commercial purposes (CDPA 1988, s.182)
   (ii) Performers are given certain property rights in their performances (CDPA 1988, ss.182A–C)
  (iii) Performers have certain right to remuneration (CDPA 1988, ss.182D and 191G)

The *sui generis* Database right

An original database may be protected as a literary work (see Chapter 7) and/or via a *sui generis* database right. Databases, therefore, have a two-level system of protection, the main features of which are compared in the following table:

Copyright protection of databases	Protection via the *sui generis* database right
Subsists in databases that are original (*i.e.* the intellectual creation of the author)	Subsists in databases whose compilation involved a substantial monetary, technical or manpower investment in obtaining, verifying or presenting the database's contents
Protects the arrangement of the data	Protects the data (contents) as infringement occurs with non-consensual extraction or re-utilisation of the whole or a substantial part of the database.
The usual copyright defences apply (see "Permitted Acts", above)	Lawful users of publicly available databases (*e.g.* subscribers) may extract and re-utilise insubstantial parts of the database for any purpose. Exceptions are also made for fair dealing, public lending and there are other defences that echo those provided for copyright in CDPA 1988, 45–50.
Full literary copyright term of protection—life of the author plus 70 years	15 years term of protection

Public lending right

Authors are entitled to compensation where their works are loaned by public libraries in order to compensate them for lost revenue from sales (see the Public Lending Rights Act 1979). The right is administered via a Public Lending Rights Scheme. It is also worth noting that in copyright, much administration of the rights is carried out by organisations known as Collecting Societies.

9. DESIGN LAW

INTRODUCTION

Designs are protected via a combination of a system of registered designs under the Registered Designs Act 1949 (as amended) and design right, with a residual role for copyright (both of the latter are governed by the CDPA 1988).

Design law—a brief history

The design regime makes little sense without some knowledge of how the present system evolved. Traditionally, copyright was an important source of protection in the design field, but a separate system of registered design was also developed to protect aesthetic designs. Before the late 1980s, there was the choice of applying (and paying for) a registered design, or, relying on copyright (which had less stringent requirements, subsisted automatically and had a longer term of protection); in such circumstances it is unsurprising that copyright was favoured. However, in some cases, *e.g. Dorling v. Honnor Marine* (1964), copyright was abused in the design field in relation to non-aesthetic designs. In *British Leyland v. Armstrong* (1986), the courts were reduced to relying on a non-IP concept, that of non-derogation from grant, to prevent copyright in spare car parts being used to develop a *de facto* monopoly in such parts.

The result was a raft of reforms in the late 1980s, which saw some reform of registered designs, the cutting back of the role of copyright in the design field and, in its place, the introduction of a new IPR for designs; the design right. More recently, in response to European developments, further reforms were introduced in 2001 to expand the registered design regime

The routes to protecting a design

Today, therefore, a design may be protected by one, or more, of:

(a) The design right (CDPA 1988, ss.213–264 (Part III)).
(b) Registered designs (Registered Designs Act 1949, as amended. Hereafter referred to as RDA 1949).
(c) Copyright, often termed "artistic copyright" (CDPA 1988, s.51–53).

The design right and registered design systems are set out below and the role of copyright is the design sphere is also briefly summarised.

THE DESIGN RIGHT

Introduction

The unregistered design right (the design right) was originally introduced to extend protection to functional designs (although it should be noted that the new registered design regime now also has a role in the protection of functional designs, see below). Design rights will automatically subsist in *both* functional and aesthetic designs, where there is:

(a) A design (as *per* CDPA 1988, s.213(2), any aspect of the shape or configuration, internal or external of the whole or part of an article).
(b) Qualification of the design (CDPA 1988, ss.213(5) and 217–221).
(c) Originality (*i.e.* not commonplace in the design field in question at the time of creation (CDPA 1988, s.213(4)).
(d) The design must be recorded (CDPA 1988, s.213(6)).
(e) The design is not excluded design, *i.e.*:
  (i) Not a method or principle of construction (CDPA 1988, s.213(3)(a)).
  (ii) Not a "must fit" feature of shape or configuration (CDPA 1988, s.213(3)(b)(i)).
  (iii) Not a "must match" feature of shape or configuration (CDPA 1988, s.213(3)(b)(ii)).
  (iv) Not a surface decoration (CDPA 1988, s.213(3)(c)).

A "design"

This is defined as "the design of any aspect of the shape or configuration (internal or external) of the whole or part of an article (CDPA 1988, s.213(2)). This means that the shape of an article (*Fulton Co. Ltd v. Grant Barnett & Co* (2000)) or its configuration, *i.e.* the way in which an article fits together (*Electronic Techniques v. Critchley* (1997)), may be protected in respect of the whole article or its constituent parts. The features of an article that are protected may be invisible to the human eye (*Ocular Sciences v. Aspect Vision Care* (1997)).

Qualification

As *per* CDPA 1988, ss.217–221, the design must qualify for protection via a "qualifying person" (a person who is a citizen or subject of a qualifying country or a person who is domiciled in a qualifying country). This person could be the designer, the commissioner of the design, the employer of the designer or the first person to market the design marketer.

Originality

A design is not original if it is commonplace in the design field in question at the time of its creation (CDPA 1988, s.213(4)). The leading case here is *Farmer's Build Limited v. Carrier Bulk Materials Handling Limited* (1999), where it was commented that a design had to be original in the sense that it is the independent work of the designer. The court set out a restrictive approach to the concept of "commonplace", but made it clear that it is not a test of novelty. In deciding whether the design of an article is commonplace, and therefore not original, the following should be noted:

   (i) The design must not have been copied from the design of an earlier article.

  (ii) The design should be *compared* with the design of contemporaneous articles produced by other parties *in the same field*, in order to ascertain similarities. This comparative exercise must be conducted objectively and in the light of the evidence, including evidence from experts in the relevant field.

 (iii) This comparison is one of fact and degree. The closer the similarity of the various designs, the more likely it is that the design is commonplace. However, where aspects of the claimant's design are only to be found in the defendant's design, the court is entitled to conclude that the design in question is not commonplace.

Recordal

For the design right to subsist, the design must be recorded either as a model or as a design document. Oral disclosure of the design, therefore, would be insufficient.

Exclusions

The following are excluded from the ambit of the design right:

(i) Methods or principles of construction (CDPA 1988, s.213(3)(a)). Design rights do not subsist in methods or principle of construction.

(ii) "Must fit" designs are excluded, *i.e.* design rights will not subsist in "features of shape or configuration of an article which enable the article to be connected to, placed in, around or against, another article so that either article can perform its function" (CDPA 1988, s.213(3)(b)(i)). Hence, design features that allow the article to interface, link, connect or otherwise physically relate to another article are excluded. "Must fit" has been held to extend to features that relate to the human body, such as contact lenses (*Ocular Science v. Aspect Vision Care* (1997)). A plug that is to interface with a socket would also be caught (*Amoena v. Trulife* (1995)).

(iii) "Must match" designs are excluded, *i.e.* design rights will not subsist in "features of shape or configuration which are dependent upon the appearance of another article of which the article is intended by the designer to form an integral part (CDPA 1988, s.213(3)(b)(ii)). Therefore, any features which need to be made in a certain way for aesthetic reasons (*e.g.* see *Mark Wilkinson Furniture v. Woodcraft Designs* (1998). Car body panels would also be excluded under "must match") would be excluded.

(iv) Surface decoration (CDPA 1988, s.213(3)(c)). Design rights do not subsist in surface decoration such as a paint finish or beading on the surface of an article (*Mark Wilkinson Furniture v. Woodcraft Designs* (1998)).

The "must fit" and "must match" exclusions were primarily intended to limit the registration of spare parts. "Must fit" related to functional considerations and "must match" is an aesthetic version of the "must fit" exclusion.

Ownership

The designer is the first owner of an unregistered design (CDPA 1988, s.215(1)), unless:

(i) The design was commissioned. Here the commissioner is the first owner (CDPA 1988, s.215(2)).
(ii) The design was made in the course of employment. Here the employer is the first owner (CDPA 1988, s.215(3)).
(iii) Where the design right subsists via qualification with reference to the first marketer of the design, that person is the first owner (CDPA 1988, s.215(4)).

Rights of the design right owner

The design right owner has the exclusive right to reproduce (copy) the design for commercial purposes by making articles to the design or making design documents CDPA 1988, s.226(1). In the context of design rights, CDPA 1988, s.226(2) requires that copying be proved (*e.g.* see *Amoena v. Trulife* (1995)). The allegedly infringing article (or design document) is to be made the same, or be *substantially the same*, to the protected design. This is an objective test to be decided by the judge through the eyes of the person to whom the design is directed *(CH Engineering v. Klucznic* (1992)).

Primary infringement

It constitutes infringement for any person to engage in the following for commercial purposes (or to purport to authorise such activity) without the permission of the design right owner (CDPA 1988, s.226):

(i) To copy the design; and
(ii) Then produce articles or design documents that are identical or substantially similar to the design.

Secondary infringement

Secondary infringement occurs where, without the permission of the design right owner, infringing articles are imported or dealt with (*e.g.* selling infringing articles), where that person knows or has reason to believe that the article is infringing (CDPA 1988, s.227(1)).

Exceptions

The following exceptions to infringement are provided:

(i) Where copyright subsists in a work in which a design right also subsists, it is not an infringement of the design right to do anything that constitutes copyright infringement in the work (CDPA 1988, s.236);

(ii) Any person is entitled to a "license of right" in the last five years of the design right (CDPA 1988, s.237);

(iii) There is a specific provision for Crown use of designs (CDPA 1988, s.240).

Duration of the design right

The design right subsists from the date upon which the design is recorded or an article is made to the design (CDPA 1988, s.213(6)). Where an article made to the design is sold within five years of the end of the first calendar year from that date, the right will subsist for ten years from the end of the year of first marketing (CDPA 1988, s.216(1)(b)). Otherwise, the right endures for fifteen years from the date on which the design is recorded in a design document or in an article (CDPA 1988, s.216(1)(a)).

During the final five years, "licenses of right" may be available to third parties (CDPA 1988, ss.237–239).

Remedies

Remedies are discussed in general in Chapter 2. The following remedies are available for design right infringement:

(i) Damages (CDPA 1988, s.229(2), but damages are not available against an innocent primary infringer (CDPA 1988, s.233) and against the innocent secondary infringer only damages of a reasonable royalty may be awarded (CDPA 1988, s.233). However, additional damages are also available (CDPA 1988, s.229(3));

(ii) Injunctions (CDPA 1988, s.229(2));

(iii) Account of profits (CDPA 1988, s.229(2));

(iv) An order for delivery up (CDPA 1988, s.230);

(v) An order for disposal (CDPA 1988, s.231);

(vi) There is a provision for groundless threat of infringement proceedings (CDPA 1988, s.253).

REGISTERED DESIGNS

Introduction

The registered designs regime underwent substantial reform in December 2001 in order to implement the Directive on the Legal Protection of Designs (Directive 98/71/EC). The Directive is intended to harmonise the laws of EU member states and it paves the way for further Community design harmonisation.

The following may be registered under the RDA 1949:

(a) A "design" (as *per* RDA 1949, s.1(2), which refers to various aspects of the appearance of the whole or part of a product).

(b) That is novel (RDA 1949, ss.1(A)(2) and 1(B)(1),(2), (5) and (6)).

(c) That has individual character (RDA 1949, s.1B(1)(3) and (4)), and

(d) Does not fall into any of the exceptions to registration:

   (i) Is not a component part of a "complex product" (RDA 1949, s.1(3)) that is not visible during normal use (RDA 1949, s.1B(8)).

   (ii) Is not a feature solely dictated by technical function (RDA 1949, s.1C(1)).

   (iii) Is not a "must fit" design (RDA 1949, s.1C(2) and (3)).

   (iv) Is not a design contrary to public policy or the accepted principles of morality (RDA 1949, s.1D).

How has the law changed?

Key changes have been made to validity, with the effect that there is a vast increase in the number of things that are registrable. For example, as graphic symbols are now registrable, greater interplay between the law of registered designs and trade mark law can be envisaged, although prior trade marks cannot, of course, be registered as designs. Stricter registration requirements, such a more stringent definition of novelty, have been introduced. The introduction of a twelve month grace period and the reform of infringement (to the advantage of the proprietor of a registered design) are other features of the new regime, with the result that registered design protection, previously rather neglected in practice, is now a very attractive option. As the UK Patent Office has indicated that it will continue with its previous practice of not examining applications with reference to prior art; this means that registered designs potentially offer a speedy and inexpensive form of protection to a wide range of products.

The old regime will continue to apply to all registrations and pending applications existing before December 9, 2001 ("pre-2001 registered designs"), but the new law will apply to the scope of registration and to infringement. However, acts that would not have constituted infringement under the old law will still be permitted in relation to such pre-2001 designs.

Hereafter, this chapter refers to the new registered design regime only. Our understanding of this new regime will increase over the next few years as case law develops. Also, there is likely to be an increasing European influence as a Community designs regime develops.

"Design"

The RDA 1949 defines a design as "the *appearance* of the *whole or part* of a *product* resulting from the features of, in particular, the lines, contours, colours, shape, texture or materials of the product or its ornamentation" (RDA 1949, s.1(2)). *Any* aspect of the appearance of a product (or the entire product) are, therefore, potentially registrable. Aesthetic designs are clearly protectable, but functional designs will also be protected provided that they are not *solely* dictated by technical function (RDA 1949, s.1C(1)).

"Product" is defined as "any industrial or handicraft item *other than a computer program*". The definition includes get up and packaging and, more significantly, graphic symbols and typefaces (RDA 1949, s.1(3)). This means that:

 (i) Handicraft items, such as craft jewelry, will now be eligible for registration.

 (ii) Significantly, the Act specifically expands protection to include graphic symbols. This means that graphic works, for example logos and character drawings, may be registrable. Potentially, trade marks could be registered as designs as a prelude to trade mark registration. Also, design registration may play a role in the protection of character merchandising.

(iii) Protection is specifically extended to get up, packaging and typefaces.

(iv) Whilst computer programs not registrable, aspects of the appearance of computer programs, such as computer icons, may well be (see *Apple Computer Inc v. Design*

Registry (2001), which although decided under the old Act, makes this clear).

Novelty

RDA 1949, s.1B provides that a design is new if no identical design or those differing only in immaterial details has been made available to the public before the date of the application for the registered design (RDA 1949, s.1A(3)). The novelty rule takes the form of a qualified type of global novelty (RDA 1949, ss.1(B)(5) and (6)); a design is novel where, at the application date, it could not have been known to commercial persons in the European Economic Area, specialising in the relevant sector. This is subject to a twelve-month grace period (RDA 1949, s.1B(6)(d)).

Individual character

In addition to novelty, a design must have individual character (RDA 1949, s.1B). A design will be considered to have individual character if, "the overall impression it produces on the informed user differs from the overall impression produced on a user by an earlier design" (RDA 1949, s.1B(3)). In assessing whether the design has this quality, the degree of freedom of the designer in developing the design is to be taken into consideration (RDA 1949, s.1B(4)).

Exceptions to registration

The main exceptions are as follows:

(a) Component part of a complex product that are not visible during normal use may not be registered (RDA 1949, s.1B(8)). "Complex product" is defined in RDA 1949, s.1(3) as "a product composed of at least two replaceable parts permitting the dis-assembly and re-assembly of the product". In effect, s.1B(8) provides that spare parts not visible during normal use (*e.g.* car engine parts) are not registrable, but those which are visible during normal use (*e.g.* car panels or bumpers) may be registered.

(b) Feature that are solely dictated by technical function are not registrable (RDA 1949, s.1C(1)). Purely functional designs are, therefore, not registrable.

(c) "Must fit" designs are not registrable. This is a limited "must fit" provision, similar, but not the same to that for the design right. In registered designs "features of shape that are required for the product in which the design is incorporated or to which it is applied to be mechanically connected to or placed in, around or against, another product so that either product may perform its function" may not be registered (RDA 1949, s.1C(2)). This exclusion does not extend to modular systems, *e.g.* stacking chairs or Lego bricks (RDA 1949, s.1C(3)).

(d) Designs contrary to public policy or the accepted principles of morality are not registrable (RDA 1949, s.1D).

Ownership

The designer is the first owner of a registered design, unless the design was commissioned, in which case the commissioner is the first owner, or created in the course of employment, here the employer would be the first owner (RDA 1949, s.2).

Cancellation of registrations

A registered design may be cancelled by the registrar upon the successful application for a declaration of invalidity (RDA 1949, s.11). Any person may make an application for a declaration of invalidity (RDA 1949, s.11ZB) and the grounds for invalidity include:

(i) The design does not satisfy one or more of the requirements of RDA 1949, s.1A(1)(a) or (b), *i.e.* there is not a novel design with individual character, or it is a design dictated by technical function, a "must fit" design, or a design contrary to public policy or immorality

(ii) It is a design excluded by RDA 1949, schedule A1 (*e.g.* a registration will be cancelled where the design utilises, without consent, devices or emblems connected to royalty or the Olympic symbol)

(iii) It is caught by the provisions relating to prior trade mark rights or copyright (RDA 1949, s.11A(3) and (4).

Rights of the registered design owner

The proprietor of a registered design has the exclusive right to use the design, or any design which does not produce on the informed user a different overall impression (RDA 1949, s.7), *i.e.* *any* product incorporating a registered design may infringe the registration and it is irrelevant as to whether the infringer has copied the registered design.

"Use" covers a wide range of scenarios, including importing or stocking a product made to the design (see RDA 1949, s.7(2)).

Infringement

Once granted, protection begins on the date of filing (RDA 1949, ss.3C(1), 7(6) and 8(1)) and is renewable every five years up to twenty-five years (RDA 1949, s.8).

A registered design will be infringed where (RDA 1949, s.7A) a person carries out any of the rights exclusive to the registered proprietor (see above), without the consent of the proprietor.

Exceptions

Exceptions to infringement include:
   (i) Private and non-commercial use of the design (RDA 1949, s.7A(2)(a)).
  (ii) Experimental use of the design (RDA 1949, s.7A(2)(b)).
 (iii) Reproducing the design for teaching purposes, subject to some qualifications (RDA 1949, s.7A(2)(c)).
  (iv) There are specific exclusions relating to ships or aircraft registered in a third country but temporarily in the UK (RDA 1949, s.7A(2)(d)–(f)).
   (v) Exhaustion within the EEA (RDA 1949, s.7A(4)).
  (vi) Certain acts relating to spare parts, see "The protection of spare parts", below (RDA 1949, s.7A(5)).
 (vii) No proceedings maybe brought for acts committed before the grant of the certificate of registration (RDA 1949, s.7(6)).
(viii) Crown use of the design (RDA 1949, s.12).

The protection of spare parts

The issue of spare parts has bedevilled design law for some time (*e.g. see British Leyland v. Armstrong* (1986)) and has not yet been the subject of European harmonisation. The Commission is obliged to commission a report on the spare parts issue at the end of 2004, in order to be able to propose amendments to European Law within a further twelve months.

There is some scope now for the registration of spare parts as registered designs. Importantly, while there is a "must fit" exclusion (RDA 1949, s.1C(2) and (3)), there is no "must match" exclusion in registered design law, but this is mitigated by the fact that there is no protection for spare parts used to restore appearance (RDA 1949, s.7A(5)), so whilst such parts could be registered, they cannot be enforced. This (along with exclusions from registrability relating to "complex product" in RDA s.1B(8) and the exclusion of purely functional designs by (RDA 1949, s.1C(1)) should help limit proprietors' ability to use registered design law to establish a monopoly in spare parts.

Remedies

Remedies are discussed in general in Chapter 2, most of the remedies discussed in that chapter should be available for registered design infringement, including:

   (i) Damages. However, no damages may be awarded against innocent infringer (RDA 1949, s.9).
   (ii) Injunctions.
   (iii) Account of profits.
   (iv) There is a provision for groundless threat of infringement (RDA 1949, s.26).

ARTISTIC COPYRIGHT

Scope of protection

In effect, only original design articles and design documents may only be protected by copyright law as artistic works (*e.g.* as sculptures or works of artistic craftsmanship). You should refer to Chapters 7 and 8 for general information about copyright law, this section only refers to provisions specific to copyright in the design field.

CDPA 1988, ss.51–52 limits the role of copyright in the design field. Copyright will not subsist in the following:

   (i) Articles and design documents other than artistic works (CDPA 1988, 51(1)).
   (ii) Where an article is made to the design/ copy article made from design (CDPA 1988, s.51).

The duration of copyright in the design field may be limited (CDPA 1988, s.52), being:

(i) Life of the author plus 70 years or,

(ii) Where the design is applied industrially (*i.e.* more than fifty copies are made) the copyright term in the industrial design field is limited to 25 years from the date of first marketing. Some things are excluded from this (CDPA 1988, s.52(4)(b)) and therefore attract the full copyright term of life plus 70 years, such as sculptures, medals and printed matter of primarily an artistic or literary character.

10. EXAMINATION CHECKLIST

N.B. These questions generally follow the order in which topics appear in this book. But not all of them do. In particular, some issues may require discussion of more than one IPR, e.g. patent questions may involve breach of confidence issues and trade mark issues might also require consideration of passing off.

1. What rights are included in the concept of "intellectual property law"?
2. What non-pecuniary remedies are available for IP infringement?
3. What is meant by "account of profits"?
4. On what basis is an account calculated?
5. What is the rule as to availability of damages?
6. Damages and account of profits are examples of pecuniary final remedies, list the non-pecuniary final remedies.
7. What is a Norwich Pharmacal Order?
8. How is *Microsoft v. Plato* (1999) significant in respect of final injunctions?
9. What is the test for the availability of an interim injunction?
10. There are two remedies available in proceedings without notice that are particularly useful in IP law, what are these and on what grounds are they available?
11. What criminal sanctions are available in IP law?
12. What is meant by a "threats action"?

13. The PA 1977 sets out the substantive criteria of patentability, what are these?
14. What things are not *inventions* "*as such*"?
15. The concept of "technical effect" is important in what part of patent law? Explain what this concept is and how it is used.
16. Are business methods patentable?
17. What is meant by a non-patentable invention?
18. What does *anticipation* mean?
19. What is the novelty test?
20. What is the "priority date" and why it is significant in the patent system?
21. Some new uses can still be novel. What are these new uses and what authority is there for their being novel?
22. What does *non-obviousness* mean?
23. The "skilled man" is relevant to obviousness—how? And, what are his attributes?
24. What is the statutory test for inventive step? What is the significance of the *Windsurfer* test in this contest?
25. So-called secondary considerations are relevant to obviousness. Explain how this is the case and gives examples of secondary considerations.
26. Discuss what is meant by *industrial application*.
27. To whom may a patent be granted?
28. Can employee inventors own inventions made during the course of employment?
29. Can employee inventors be compensated?
30. "Sufficiency" is an important concept in patent law. What does it mean?
31. List the acts that constitute patent infringement.
32. Are there any exceptions to infringement?
33. On what grounds may a patent be revoked?
34. Claim interpretation is a key element of patent infringement. Explain what is meant by "claim interpretation", why it is important and what is the significance of *Wheatly v. Drillsafe* (2001).
35. What remedies are available for patent infringement?
36. What impact has the Human Rights Act 1998 had on breach of confidence?
37. *Coco v. Clarke* (1969) is a significant breach of confidence case—why?
38. What constitutes information with the *necessary quality of confidence*?

39. What circumstances give rise to an *obligation of confidence*?
40. The position of the current employee differs from that of the ex-employee when it comes to implying an obligation of confidence. What is the difference between current and ex-employees in this area?
41. Are third parties who receive confidential information, bound by an obligation of confidence?
42. What constitutes *use of confidential information*?
43. Is intent relevant to use?
44. Subconscious use does not breach the obligation of confidence—true or false?
45. What defences are available against an action for breach of confidence?
46. What remedies are available for an action for breach of confidence?
47. What is the function of a trade mark? What are collective and certification marks and how do they differ from ordinary trade marks?
48. *Absolute grounds for refusal* are concerned with a conflict based on third party rights—true or false?
49. *Relative grounds for refusal* are concerned with objections based on the mark itself—true or false?
50. What is the Nice Agreement?
51. Define a "trade mark".
52. Set out the absolute and relative grounds for refusal.
53. How can one graphically represent a scent mark?
54. There is a proviso to TMA 1994 s.3(1). What is it?
55. Explain what a mark devoid of distinctive character is.
56. Can an exclusively descriptive sign be registered as a trademark?
57. What is meant by a generic sign?
58. The TMA 1994 has special provision for shape marks. What are these and how is the ECJ's judgment in *Philips v. Remington* significant?
59. When will a mark be immoral?
60. What constitutes a deceptive mark?
61. What is an "earlier trade mark"?
62. What is the scope of "honest concurrent use"?
63. What constitutes an "identical mark"?
64. The concept of confusing similarity is important both to the relative grounds for refusal (*i.e.* TMA 1994, s.5(2)), but also to infringement (*i.e.* TMA 1994, s.10(2)). What is does "confusion" mean?
65. When will conflict with a mark of repute be a valid ground upon which to refuse registration?

66. On what grounds may a mark be revoked?
67. What acts constitute trade mark infringement?
68. Some defences to trade mark infringement are available. What are they?
69. What remedies are available for trade mark infringement?
70. Certain criminal offences are relevant to trade mark law— what are these?
71. What are the elements for the action of passing off as set out in *Jif Lemon* (1990)? Is there an alternative formulation? Which do you prefer?
72. How would you define "goodwill"? Why are territorial considerations important?
73. What actions might constitute an actionable misrepresentation in passing off?
74. Various forms of damage may result from the misrepresentation, list these.
75. What defences and remedies are available to an action of passing off?
76. What is the main UK authority on cybersquatting?
77. Is passing off helpful in endorsement, sponsorship or character merchandising?
78. Is deception required for a successful action in passing off?
79. The CDPA 1988 sets out the conditions that have to be satisfied before copyright will subsist, what are these?
80. List the primary copyright works.
81. List the secondary copyright works.
82. Describe the significance of *Norowzian v. Arks (No. 2)* (1999).
83. What role (if any) does artistic merit have for artistic works?
84. What is the test used to determine whether a work is a work of artistic craftsmanship?
85. Identify the copyright works that subsist in the following: the website of a national newspaper, a CD compilation of popular songs, an episode of a BBC soap opera, a cartoon, and, the soundtrack of a Hollywood movie. Please bear in mind that multiple copyrights may subsist in any one real world object.
86. What is meant by "the idea/expression dichotomy"?
87. Which copyright works must be original? What is meant by an "original work"?
88. Are there other standards of originality?
89. Artistic works are subject to the requirement of fixation— true or false?

90. Who is the author of a copyright work?
91. Who is the first owner of a copyright work?
92. When will joint ownership of a copyright work occur?
93. When is an employer the first owner of copyright?
94. What are the two forms of copyright infringement?
95. What are the exclusive rights of the copyright owner?
96. What does "taking the whole or a substantial part" of a work mean and why is this requirement significant?
97. Define what acts constitute infringement of the reproduction right.
98. What acts constitute secondary infringement?
99. Set out the main "permitted acts".
100. Fair dealing in a copyright work is allowed for any purpose—true or false?
101. If a film-maker deliberately includes a musical work in his film, this will not constitute copyright infringement because of the provisions on incidental inclusion—true or false?
102. Decompiling a computer program can not constitute copyright infringement—true or false?
103. What remedies are available for copyright infringement?
104. What are moral rights?
105. Give the duration of copyright in the following works: a computer-generated picture; the typography of a literary work in which (literary) copyright has lapsed; an unreleased sound recording that was made in 1973, and, a film.
106. Which IPRs are relevant in the design field? Which IP statutes are relevant?
107. When will the design right subsist?
108. Define a "design" under the design right legislation.
109. When will a design qualify for design right protection?
110. What is meant by "originality" in the context of design rights? (You might also consider how it differs to the originality requirement in copyright law).
111. Explain the main exclusions from the design right. In particular, what is meant by "must fit" and "must match"?
112. Explain the ownership rules for unregistered designs.
113. What constitutes infringement of the design right? What are the exceptions to infringement?
114. What is the duration of the design right?
115. What remedies are available for design right infringement?
116. What are the registrability requirements for registered designs?

117. Are the following "designs" within the meaning of the RDA 1949: A cartoon character, grooves on a milk container, computer icons, and, a handmade earring?
118. What is meant by "novelty" under the RDA 1949? (You might also consider how it differs to novelty in patent law)
119. When will a design have "individual character" under the RDA 1949?
120. Explain the main exceptions to registration under the RDA 1949, in particular, explaining the "must fit" exclusion.
121. What acts constitute infringement of a registered design? What are the exceptions to infringement (in particular, explain RDA 1949, s.7A(5))?
122. What would be the duration of copyright in an industrially applied design?

---

11. SAMPLE QUESTIONS AND MODEL ANSWERS

THE EXAMINATION

The golden rule for most law examinations would be to "answer the *question*; *all* of the question (*i.e.* all it's constituent parts) and nothing but the question" (*i.e.* do not digress, keep your answer relevant to the question). Preparation, revision, practice and planning all have a role in this.

Preparation

Most IP examinations require candidates to answer problem and essay questions. The format and style of examinations and the rubric, of course, varies between institutions, as may the syllabus. Students are strongly advised to study their course syllabus and any relevant examination regulations.

If possible, obtain and study past papers. The purpose of this is not to facilitate "question spotting" (a dangerous practice, as past papers cannot be regarded as providing an accurate guide to questions that will be included in the forthcoming examination), but rather to ensure that you are familiar with the format and style of the examination, and, in order to facilitate practice (see below).

Revision

By now you should be aware of the revision methods that you find to be most effective. Students should try to ensure that they have adequate time for revision.

Practice

Too many candidates make the mistake of revising, revising and revising, and the first time they attempt to apply their hard-won knowledge and understanding is in the examination. As most IP examinations assess your ability to analyse and discuss issues within a limited period of time, it makes sense to practice this skill as part of your revision by answering questions from past papers. If you do this in good time, your course lecturer or tutor may be prepared to mark or comment on your practice answers.

Planning

During the examination, it is often advisable to plan your answers. Planning is conducive to structured and clear work.

ESSAY QUESTIONS

Essay questions can often be answered in different ways, depending on the candidate's views. Nevertheless, you must set out what the relevant law is as well as putting forward your arguments (considering the merits of opposing views is also helpful), making reference to authority and, for the statutory IPRs, the relevant statutes. Pay some attention to the structure of your answer; it is surprising how many candidates in exam conditions forget that essays should have a beginning (a short introduction) a middle (what the relevant law is and relevant arguments) and an end (a conclusion).

Sample question

"Morality and public policy have no role to play in the patent system." Discuss.

Sample answer

This is an essay question that could, potentially, be answered in a wide range of ways and the topic can generate very strong views. Nevertheless, candidates should be wary of writing an answer with "too much opinion and not enough law". The starting point should be the PA 1977, s.1(3), which provides that where the commercial exploitation of an invention is contrary to public policy or morality, the invention is unpatentable, morality clearly has *some* role to play in the patent system. However, that role may be a very small one, depending on one's interpretation of the decisions of the EPO in this area, and the question remains: *should* there be a role in the patent system for public policy considerations and morality?

Candidates should be aware from their wider reading that this has been a controversial area, particularly in relation to biotechnological inventions. This is evidenced by the fact that the Directive on the Legal Protection of Biotechnological Inventions (98/44/EC) took such a long time to come to fruition. The Directive has been incorporated into UK Law via PA 1977, Schedule A2. This essentially summarises EPO jurisprudence on moral and public policy concerns in relation to biotechnological inventions, and candidates would probably make some critical comments on this in their answer (*e.g.* should human germ line therapy be excluded? Do the provisions relating to plant and animal varieties set out a reasonable position?)

As the essay question is not limited to biotechnological inventions, however, the candidate should describe and analyse general EPO and UK jurisprudence on morality and public policy. Candidates might be aware from their wider reading of some UK cases on morality and if so, might discuss these (*e.g. Riddlesbarger* (1936), *Schering* (1971) and *Organon* (1970)). These were not included in Chapter 3 as these were decided under the old patent regime. Emphasis should instead be placed on analysing relevant decisions of the EPO (as these would be more relevant under the PA 1977), such as *NOVARTIS/Transgenic plant* (1999) and *Harvard OncoMouse* (1990).

It is difficult to be prescriptive as to how candidates might approach an analysis of EPO jurisprudence on these issues, as so much depends on the individual candidate's opinion. Certainly he/she should consider discussing the extent to which plant and animal varieties are patentable, bearing in mind that inventions concerning plants and animals may be patentable where they are not confined to a particular variety (*NOVARTIS/Transgenic plant* (1999) and *Harvard OncoMouse* (1990)). Also, to what extent are factors such as animal suffering and environmental damage considered in the patenting process (see *Harvard OncoMouse* (1990))?

Following this analysis, candidates should conclude by coming to some view as to the extent that morals and public policy considerations will be considered in UK the patent process. If they disagree with this position, candidates might also (briefly) set out recommendations for reform.

PROBLEM QUESTIONS

Problem questions largely dictate the structure of answers, for example you can structure your answer by issue or by party, as appropriate. A useful rule of thumb in planning an answer to a problem question is to question the significance of all the information provided in the question. Unless your examiner is fond of red herrings, it is likely that descriptions, events, dates, actions etc., are all relevant.

Sample question

James is a stand-up comedian with a talent for improvisation. As part of his act, he asks the audience for themes and styles for songs which he then improvises; he sings and accompanies himself on a piano. When James is performing at the StarStruck Club, the owner of the club allows two members, of the audience, Gill and Grant, to record James. James does not give permission for this.

Gill and Grant then make two hundred copies of James' improvised songs. These are sold to Fidgets, a respectable music shop. Fidgets put the tapes on sale and play one of the tapes over the shop's sound system to encourage customers to purchase it.

One of these customers is Phillip, an aspiring novelist. Philip is so inspired by "Rejection", one of James' improvised songs which describes a blind date gone wrong, that he writes a 500 page novel (called "Rejection") based on the incident as it is described in this two minute song. This novel is to be published next month. Phillip has called the foolish male protagonist in his novel "James".

Advise James.

Sample answer

This problem question raises a wide range of copyright issues. Relevant case law and statutory authority should be cited in addressing these points, which include:

(a) Do any copyright works subsist in James' performance? Yes, copyright is likely to subsist in James' songs as original literary (CDPA 1988, s.3(1)) and musical (CDPA 1988, s.3(1)(a)) works. Such works must be fixed (CDPA 1988, s.3(2)), but Gill and Grant have fixed the work via their recording (CDPA 1988, s.3(3)). The qualification requirement is also met. Copyright will also subsist in the recording that Gill and Grant have made (but who will own this?). Candidates might also briefly consider the position as to performers' rights.

As suggestions for the songs came from the audience, is James the author of the literary and musical works that subsist in these songs? *Wiseman v. George Weidenfeld and Nicholson Ltd and Donaldson* (1985) suggest that merely supplying ideas would be insufficient for members of the audience to be considered as joint authors and the test suggested in *Cala Homes* (1995) has not been met, so James is probably the author. James is, therefore, likely to be the first owner of the copyrights in the songs (unless he is an employee of the StarStruck Club). If James has not assigned or licensed his rights, he will be able to enforce the economic rights in these works (*i.e.* he will be able to bring proceedings for primary and secondary infringement, as appropriate). In either case, as the author James will also have certain moral rights in relation to these copyright works.

(b) What is the position of the owner of the StarStruck Club? Has the owner authorised Gill and Grant's activities? If so, analysis of *CBS v. Amstrad* (1988) is necessary in order to assess whether he/she has authorised infringement (CDPA 1988, s.16(2)). Certainly it seems that he/she knew of Gill and Grant's activities, so the candidate should consider whether the owner's actions fall within CDPA 1988, s.25. Candidates should consider whether the club owner might benefit from any of the permitted acts (this is unlikely) and what remedies (if any) that James may have against the club owner.

(c) What is the position of Gill and Grant? Their activities are likely to constitute a range of primary and secondary infringements. For example, there is infringement of the reproduction right (CDPA 1988, s.17(2)) as well as the distribution right (CDPA 1988, s.18) and public performance rights (s.19). Candidates might refer to cases such as *Ladbroke v. William Hill* (1964) and *Infabrics v. Jaytex* (1982) in their analysis here. Candidates should also consider the position as to secondary infringement, in particular CDPA 1988, s.23–24, and performers' rights.

Will any of the permitted acts be relevant? Recording without permission and selling these recordings is unlikely to constitute fair dealing for any of the permitted purposes (CDPA 1988, ss.29–30) and no other permitted act appears relevant, for example, the public interest defence does not apply to Gill and Grant's activities. Candidates should therefore consider what remedies might be relevant. James might press for additional damages (CDPA 1988, s.97(2)), as well as a prohibitory injunction to prevent further copies of the songs being made. There may be some scope for criminal sanctions via CDPA 1988, ss.107–8.

(d) The position of the music shop, Fidgets. Candidates should consider any relevant secondary infringements here. The issue of *mens rea* will be crucial to establishing infringement here. Again, any remedies that may be available to James should be noted.

(e) What is the position of Phillip—does Phillip's book infringe the literary copyright in James' song? Can James prevent Philip from calling the book's main character "James"? In relation to the first question, there is unlikely to be sufficient originality in the title "Rejection" for copyright to subsist (alternatively, one could argue that the *de minimis* principle applies here, as in *Exxon Corporation v. Exxon Ind.* (1982)). However, discussion of infringement and the idea/expression dichotomy is germane to the issue of whether a 500-page book based on a two minute song can constitute infringement of the literary copyright subsisting in that: the "plot" would surely be tantamount to a non-protected idea (*e.g. Green v. New Zealand Broadcasting Corporation* (1989)) and it is unlikely to constitute a "substantial taking" (see *Ladbroke v. William Hill* (1964), *Hawkes v. Paramount Films* (1934) and *Bauman v. Fussell* (1953)). Relevant infringements and remedies should be set out. The candidate might also briefly consider whether James can prevent Philip from calling the book's main character "James"—this is unlikely to be possible under copyright law.

INDEX